IBSEN STUDIES

IBSEN STUDIES

BY

P. J. EIKELAND, A.M., LITT.D.

Professor of Norwegian
St. Olaf College

———

Edited by a Committee

of the

Language Group
St. Olaf College

HASKELL HOUSE PUBLISHERS Ltd.
Publishers of Scarce Scholarly Books
NEW YORK. N. Y. 10012

First Published 1934

HASKELL HOUSE PUBLISHERS Ltd.
Publishers of Scarce Scholarly Books
280 LAFAYETTE STREET
NEW YORK, N. Y. 10012

Library of Congress Catalog Card Number: 76-117595

Standard Book Number 8383-1028-1

Printed in the United States of America

PREFACE

The four articles included in this volume were written by Professor P. J. Eikeland at various times during his long period of service as head of the Department of Norwegian at St. Olaf College.

Three of the essays have been printed before:

Peer Gynt was published in *Symra*, vol. 8, 1912, pp. 136-159.

Brand: (Spredte Bemerkninger om Ibsen; Ibsens Brand) was printed in *Teologisk Tidsskrift*, vol. IV., October, 1920.

The Pretenders formed the Introduction of *Holvik and Eikeland's* edition of *Kongsemnerne*, published in 1916.

The Pillars of Society has not been published before. The manuscript of this article was found among Professor Eikeland's papers after his death, which occurred in 1927.

All the articles were written in Norwegian and are in substance lectures delivered before his classes in Norwegian Literature.

The late Professor O. E. Rølvaag became Dr. Eikeland's colleague and successor in the Department of Norwegian. Dr. Rølvaag thought that these essays deserved to be made available to a larger group of readers than those for whom they were composed originally. This would only be possible if they were translated into English and offered to the public through the regular channels. Taking the initiative in the matter he suggested to the Language Group of the faculty of St. Olaf College that this body become the sponsors of the translation and publication of the articles. At a meeting of the Group in the fall of 1930 the proposition was agreed to. A committee headed by Professor Rølvaag was elected to have charge of the undertaking. Translators were secured and the work was begun immediately. The sudden death of Professor Rølvaag in November, 1931, delayed the matter for some time. Other causes, not the least of which was the present financial depression, created difficulties. The committee continued its efforts, however, and the volume is now offered to the public.

The sponsors of the articles in their English garb offer no apology for their publication. The reason for their appearance is to be sought in the essays themselves and in the continued and widespread interest in Ibsen. Nor do we pretend to offer any estimate of their value. They must stand or fall on their merits. Professor Eikeland was recognized as a scholar of sound judgment, a thorough student of Ibsen. Himself a Norwegian, with a profound knowledge of Norse history and of the social conditions and problems with which the plays of Ibsen deal, he was competent to express opinions of his own and to judge critically the opinions of others. That in his criticism he perhaps at times approaches the subject from a viewpoint different from that of other critics, should not lessen the value of his observations.

The committee desires to express its appreciation to the family of Professor Eikeland and to the Augsburg Publishing House for permission to publish the articles; also to the many who by financial assistance and interest have helped to make possible the publication of the volume.

The editorial committee: Marie Malmin Meyer, Arthur C. Paulson, J. Jørgen Thompson, Nils Flaten.

—N. F.

St. Olaf College,
Northfield, Minn.,
March, 1934.

CONTENTS

IBSEN STUDIES

PEER GYNT
  Translated by ARTHUR C. PAULSON, PH.D.

The PRETENDERS
  Translated by NILS FLATEN, PH.D.

BRAND
  Translated by MARIE MALMIN MEYER, PH.D.

The PILLARS OF SOCIETY
  Translated by OLAV LEE, M.A.

PEER GYNT

Like the fabled fishing pool of the Norwegian "hulder," much of what Ibsen has written has two depths. On the surface certain things are in evidence, but if we plunge deeper, we may discover other things so different from those on the surface as to be scarcely recognizable. As Just Bing has said, in reading Ibsen we must constantly be on guard for hidden meanings. This is true, not only in his later works where the symbolic is obvious, but in his earlier works as well. He usually has something "up his sleeve." For example, there are times when smug and self righteous we sit reading in Ibsen about hideous creatures which we can scarcely believe exist, at least not in our particular section of the world, only to discover that we are seeing a veritable portrait of ourselves, smugness and all.

In *Peer Gynt* this truth is very much in evidence.

I hear many people saying: "Peer Gynt! I should say not! We may be degenerate enough, goodness knows, but we are not Peer Gynts. Far from it!"

No, perhaps not. At least not the Peer Gynt who rides the reindeer-buck along the Gendin Ridge, who fights with Aslak Smith, or who tosses his mother to the roof of the mill house and leaves her there. But Peer Gynt is an elusive fellow, and when we think we are most rid of him, we find him waiting for us at the next turn in the road.

"This stuff is not poetry," exclaimed Georg Brandes after he had read *Peer Gynt* for the first time.

"My work *is* poetry," roared Ibsen in reply. "And if it is not, it *shall* be."

This proud answer is interesting from two points of view. In the first place it shows that had there been a time when Ibsen doubted himself to the extent that he could see an analogy between himself and Jarl Skule of

The Pretenders, such time was past. In the second place it shows Ibsen possessing greater vision and more consummate knowledge than even the great critic of the North. For Ibsen's contention has been realized. Today no critic of any consequence would dare question the artistry inherent in *Peer Gynt*. On the contrary, most critics from the point of view of pure poetry, would give it first rank in Northern literature. Fourteen years later, Brandes himself admitted that he had been mistaken. At that time he acknowledged it "the most vigorous of Ibsen's works."

Peer Gynt, as we have said, may be approached from two angles. In my opinion this fact must be kept clearly in mind at all times, if one is to have a true understanding of its deeper significance.

X   From one point of view the protagonist, Peer Gynt, is a picture of the typical Norwegian — not as he has been since the year 1870, or as he was before the 1850's — but as he appeared to Ibsen during the decade centering upon 1860. In other words, Peer Gynt is a portrait of the Norwegian who, in Ibsen's eyes at least, had been grossly misled and befuddled by that great movement known as *Romanticism* or the *Romantic Revival*.

We must, therefore, first look at Peer Gynt as the typical Norwegian of the 1860 period, and try to understand why it is that Ibsen makes romanticism responsible for the fact that the picture he paints of his countrymen is so far from flattering.

Romanticism! But was there nothing good or great, then, in the romantic movement? There most certainly was. And I think that Ibsen himself would have been the last to disparage the many truly good and great things which the romantic movement brought to the cultural life of the people of Norway. Its effect in arousing the national consciousness was so great that it has been said with much truth that the Norwegians "moved home to themselves from a four hundred year exile" with the coming of romanticism.   Then for the first time they began to take stock of themselves and to consider the rock from which they were hewn.   Then only did they begin to investigate what they had created during the past centuries and to bring to light that which remained in such fields as folk-literature, folk-language, folk-music and the like.   When we consider, for exam. 'e, what a tremendous part the folk-literature has played in the cultural life of the Norwegian people during the last half century, it seems almost preposterous that Henrik Wergeland as late as 1840 was not aware of the existence of such folk-literature, though he was inclined to believe there was such a thing.   Then in the 40's and 50's came the discovery of that great treasure hoard of Norwegian folk-culture — a treasure which gave artists and authors of the succeeding generation both strength and inspiration.   In fact, one may almost say that it called them into being.   With this in mind we must consider it as no empty compliment what Bjørnson said to Asbjørnsen, who together with Jørgen Moe had been the pioneer of the romantic movement in Norway: "I should have been nothing but for you."   And when Norway in the three decades from 1860 to 1890 came to play a leading role on the stage of world literature, it was romanticism which was largely responsible.

But everything has two sides, and one of these is the seamy side. Romanticism, too, had its seamy side; Norwegian romanticism as well as others.   For it is characteristic of every "movement" that from the beginning it may have within itself some very definite qualities which in the course of time may bring about its downfall.   A "movement" usually begins as a reaction against some older order, and as a result the "new" is the direct antithesis of the "old."   If the "old" has gone too far in one direction, the "new" will go too far in the other.   Now we know that the romantic movement came into being as a direct reaction against neo-classicism, or as it is called in church history *rationalism;* and it would be easy to mention a number of traits that came into being as a result of this reaction. I shall, however, mention only the three that are most pertinent to this study.

Neo-classicism was a cold, intellectual movement. It would have nothing to do with the emotions or with imagination. Romanticism brought a sharp reaction to all this. Soon emotionalism — perhaps sentimentalism — and imagination were in the saddle. If, according to the precepts of neo-classicism, any Tom, Dick, or Harry who was diligent enough and studious enough could become a poet, now, under romanticism no one — as is probably true — could become a poet who was not born one. But at the same time, unfortunately, they saw no need for diligent work or for study. The "happy idler" was now the ideal. Oehlenschlæger, the pioneer of the romantic movement in Denmark, has this ideal stand forth without restriction or restraint in his first drama *Aladdin or the Wonderful Lamp.* By a stroke of fortune the lazy Aladdin gets possession of both lamp and ring, and as a result soon has the whole world at his feet; whereas Nureddin, poor fellow, in spite of life-long study and hard work gets nowhere.

Another characteristic of neo-classicism was its utter disregard and disparagement of nationalism and of the past, especially the medieval period. And here again romanticism brought a complete reversal. Now it became something great to be — not cosmopolitan — but German, English, Scotch, Danish, Norwegian. Of course in Norway, even before this time, poets had written charming verse on festive occasions about "Norway, the homeland of heroes," but hitherto, or at least up to the time Wergeland had come forward ten years earlier as an exponent of nationalism, most of the people had felt that it was more distinguished to be Danish — at

all events more satisfactory from a cultural point of
view. But now with the advent of romanticism in the
early 40's, the people began to feel that there was something noble, something distinctly splendid in being Norwegians. One of the best examples of this nationalistic
pride is the almost classic expression of Ole Bull: "Ole
Olson, Norwegian Norseman from Norway."   And the
past —

> The old unhappy far off things,
> And battles long ago;

that was the golden age, nothing less.   In *Guldhornene,*
the prelude of romanticism in the North, Oehlenschlæger has an old antiquarian offer the following prayer:

> Give us a glimpse
> Of days long forgotten,
> When the splendor of the East
> Abode in the Northland.

And the old gods heard his prayer.   They allowed two
"glimpses from the past to reach the new age" — two
golden drinking horns inscribed with runes.   By whom
were they found?   The old antiquarian?   Oh No!   One
was discovered by a beautiful young maiden, and the
other by a young peasant as he was out plowing.   As
for the horns with their runic inscriptions:

> A hidden mystery hovers over the ancient runes and symbols;
> A glory as of God crowns the mysteries of eternity.

Now the past came into its own.

Long before romanticism had gained general acceptance in Norway — it had reached there forty years later
than it reached Denmark — the Norwegians had been
enthusiastic about their ancient greatness.

> What Norway was, that she may be again
> Among all peoples, both on land and sea.

Wergeland had written as early as 1834.   That Norway
might rise to greater heights in the future than in the

past never occurred to him, apparently. With the advent of romanticism this early enthusiasm became more widespread and ardent than ever. Moreover, that which the people of Norway began to take special pride in now was the literature which had flourished from the 12th down to the 17th century — folk-tales, folk-legends, and ballads.

This was all very good and well — both that the people of Norway should admire their past greatness and that they should be proud of their folk-literature. For Norway does have a proud past. Its folk-literature, too, ranks very high. The brothers Grimm, who certainly must be considered authorities on the subject, say it is the best that can be found.

But it is of little consequence to us that our ancestors were great, if we ourselves are not. "If you cannot bend the bow, it is not yours." As for the folk-tales, we could manage very well with them if we were all Askelads and Aladdins, winning princesses and half-kingdoms by some stroke of good luck. Unfortunately, there is such a thing as our prosaic everyday life, and what takes place in fairy tales seldom takes place in the ordinary existence of an individual. What we mean is that genius, imagination, emotion and fantasy are splendid qualities, but that work, initiative, study and research are equally splendid. For there are very few of us who are geniuses, and even these few find it difficult to escape work. Oehlenschlæger himself discovered that soon enough.

It was this seamy side of romanticism which, according to Ibsen, had befuddled the Norwegian people of the 1860's. They went around thinking themselves great because their ancestors had been great. They had eyes for nothing but their ancient glory. It is in *Brand*, particularly, that Ibsen has given us a scathing portrait of this inordinate admiration for the past. With considerable naïveté and self-satisfaction the village mayor answers the inquiries of Brand.

> All has its time, each time its need,
> Each age its proper work to do;
> We also flung our mite into
> The world's great treasure of bold deed.
> True, that's long since; but, after all,
> The mite was not so very small.
> Now the land's dwindled and decay'd,
> But our renown still lives in story.
> The days of our departed glory
> Were when the great Kinge Bele swayed.

Then, after telling in detail *how* the town acquired its great fame during the reign of King Bele, the mayor continues:

> Over the blood thus set a-flowing
> There's been perhaps excessive crowing;
> But after what I've said, I may,
> I think, without a touch of vanity,
> Point backward to the stir we made
> In the great Age long since decay'd,
> And hold that we indeed have paid
> Our little mite of Fire and Fray
> Toward the Progress of Humanity.

And when Brand is audacious enough to remark that the descendants of King Bele's heroes have evidently forgotten that "Nobility is a trust," the mayor replies:

> By no means. Only go and mark
> Our parish on its gaudy nights,
> Where I with Constable and Clerk,
> And Judge preside as leading lights;
> You'll warrant, when the punch goes round,
> King Bele's memory is sound.

The memory of the king's glorious reign is enthusiastically revered, he declares, with clinking of glasses, with songs, and with toasts.

This is Ibsen's conception of what the heroic past meant to the average Norwegian during the 1860's. But in *Brand* the portrait is unfinished. In his next drama, therefore, Ibsen completes the picture and leaves no doubt in the minds of his fellow countrymen as to what he thinks of them. They are nothing but vain dreamers, visionaries, who have been so filled with folk tales and fairy stories that they no longer can distinguish between fact and fancy. Painting this portrait of Peer Gynt, he holds it before his fellow Norwegians, saying: "Now just take a look at yourselves, good people."

Peer Gynt is a farmer lad — a *bonde* or freeholder. During the 60's Ibsen had a special grudge against the *bonde* group, because its members in parliament had brought failure to his dearest wish and almost certain hope — that Norway would come to the aid of Denmark in its war with Germany in 1864. That the Norwegians and Swedes could sit quietly at home while Denmark was engaged in a bloody war of tremendous significance to all Scandinavia, was a blow that Ibsen never forgot. Therefore in *Brand*, but even more in *Peer Gynt*, he poured out his wrath in such a steady stream that we can scarcely blame the Norwegians for feeling like Peer Gynt in Act V:

> If I've had to bow 'neath the lashes of fate,
> Trust me to find folks I can lash in my turn.

They understood well enough that Peer Gynt was a picture of the whole Norwegian race, not of the *bonde* party alone. And as we said before, the portrait is certainly not flattering. But instead of chastising him, they turned out to hear his play night after night, and ended by giving him a yearly stipend. For this, at least, they should be given some credit.

But what are the traits that the average Norwegian of the 1860's had in common with Peer Gynt?

There are enough of them, certainly. They fill the whole drama from the beginning of the first act to the final curtain. But if we are to see Peer in his most significant role, we must concentrate on his most outstanding *Norwegian* traits. The first of these is that he is of good stock. His grandfather, Rasmus Gynt, was wealthy, had "bushels of money," which Peer's father, once the inheritance fell to him, soon managed to give wings. The family, therefore, has fallen on evil days.

And in such circumstances we find Peer, now grown to
manhood, wandering about day-dreaming. He is highly
conscious of his poverty, but it never occurs to him that
it might be his duty to "raise the fallen." Far from it.
In his own conceit he is able and gifted, and the future
has bright prospects for him. He even dreams of an
empire of which he shall be the ruler. It is good fortune,
however, not work that shall accomplish all this. "Fortune may falter, but it never loses its stride."

"Do you understand what I mean, good people?"
asks Ibsen. "Once you too had 'bushels of money', but
during the time of Danish overrule, your fathers wasted
what your ancestors gathered in the glorious days of the
sagas. But in spite of this, you seem smug and compla-
cent. Here you sit, glorying in the fact that you are the
descendants of these valiant Norsemen — some from
the old sea-kings themselves — and wait for a new day
of greatness. At the same time you refuse to *do* anything. You even refuse to help your brother when he is
in distress. And instead of bending every effort to
build up your homeland, you strike out for America.
There you expect to find fortune and become wealthy."

The second dominant Norwegian trait is that Peer
has been brought up on folk tales and fairy stories.
Aase, his mother, frankly admits that she and Peer
found it necessary —

> To seek in shadows what they miss in life
> A recompense of dreams to hide the truth.
>
> Oh we clung closely in sorrow and need.
> Ay, you must know that my husband he drank,
> Loafed round the parish to roister and prate,
> Wasted and trampled our gear under foot.
> And meanwhile at home sat Peerkin and I—
> The best we could do was to try to forget.
> It's a terrible thing to look fate in the eyes;
> And of course one is glad to be quit of one's cares,
> And try all one can to hold thinking aloof.
> Some take to brandy, and others to lies;
> And we — why we took to fairy tales
> Of princes and trolls and of all sorts of beasts;
> And of bride rapes as well. Ah but who could have dreamt
> That those devil yarns would have stuck in his head.

Yes, Peer was reared on fairy stories. And for the most part he continues to live in them. Dirty and ragged, he lies in the heather, watching the clouds floating overhead, and little by little gives his imagination free rein, until he sees the clouds as a glittering troop of knights with Emperor Peer in the lead.

> Women are curtseying. All the world knows him
> Kaiser Peer Gynt, and his thousands of henchmen,
> Engelland's Prince on the seashore awaits him;
> There too await him all Engelland's maidens.
> Engelland's nobles and Engelland's Kaiser,
> See him come riding and rise from their banquet.

The third significant trait is that Peer finally strikes out for America. He simply has no luck at home. Everything goes from bad to worse. In the end as a punishment for kidnapping the bride of Hegstad, he loses what little is left of his patrimony. Consequently there is nothing left for him but to seek his fortune in the New World. And once there, as he himself says:

> . . . Luck you see was kind to me;
> Old Fate, too, was accommodating.
> I prospered.

All his energies are bent toward acquiring wealth, and his conscience is never allowed to interfere with his money making.

> I made most
> In negro slaves for Carolina,
> And idol-images for China.

He has plenty of initiative and ingenuity now, but it is for the sole purpose of acquiring a huge fortune in the shortest possible time that he may "become emperor through the power of gold." As a result he heaps up a tremendous fortune. He slaps his pocket and says, "I have cash, and am myself: Sir Peer Gynt." And yet — how very poor he really is! He has no interest in the finer things of life; money is everything. He has no fatherland; no ties of any kind. America for him is the land of gold, nothing more. As for Norway, he doesn't

give it a thought for years. Yet finally, old and gray,
he returns home.

> They shall know in the parish
> That Peer has come sailing aloft o'er the sea!

He finds, however, that he is a stranger in a strange
land. He recognizes no one; no one recognizes him.
The welcome he had expected is not forthcoming.

Thus it is that in *Peer Gynt*, Ibsen has pictured for us
the typical Norwegian — or at least one aspect of him.
(And it may be that he has given us Norwegian-Ameri-
cans a little portrait of ourselves too.) Whether he is
entirely just in his portrait of the Norwegian people is,
of course, somewhat questionable. There is no doubt,
however, but that it was good for them. Fridtjof Nan-
sen, for example, gives credit for many of his exploits
to *Brand* and *Peer Gynt*. He says that they kept egging
him on to greater accomplishments. And may not the
success of the negotiations with Sweden in 1905 be
traced to the same source?

Yet had *Brand* and *Peer Gynt* given us nothing more
than a picture of the typical Norwegian of the 1860's,
they would never have attained their high position in
world literature. The chances are that they would have
been dead and forgotten long ago. It may be that *Peer
Gynt* would still be interesting to the Norwegians in
that they could see how they appeared to Ibsen seventy
years ago — especially since the work abounds in the
most delightful humor. But for a German, an Englishman, an American — in fact, for any race other than
Norwegian — that particular picture is of little consequence. An American critic speaking with respect to
this fact says: "Norse critics maintain that *Brand* represents the Norwegians as they should be; *Peer Gynt*
as they really are. That may be true. But I am interested in these works for an entirely different reason."

And we can say with Peer Gynt: "Well now, with
us it is exactly the same." To us, also, *Peer the Norwegian* is much less significant than *Peer the Man*. And

as I see it, the most delightful thing in Ibsen is that he
has succeeded so well in combining the two characters
that a Norwegian critic such as Henrik Jæger, for example, may see in Peer Gynt the typical Norwegian and
nothing more; whereas a critic of non-Norwegian stock
may see in him a perfect picture of the typical human
being.

The typical — the universal — that is exactly what
Peer is. And because he is the typical human being, he
becomes in Ibsen's eyes the typical egoist. Whatever
one may think at the present time of Ibsen's attitude
toward the Bible, or for that matter, toward Christianity
in general, with respect to its conception of the natural
man he is in complete accord. To him, also, egoism,
pride, is the root of all evil. And the way to manhood
according to Ibsen, a manhood "such as was conceived
in the mind of God," is through denial of self. He
knows no other way.

But Ibsen does not say that we are all egoists in the
same manner that Peer was. Far from it. Egoism expresses itself in various ways. It may take the form of
delight in sensuous pleasure, of passion for honor, of
lust for power, of covetousness, or possibly something
else. All these different forms, however, manifest one
common quality — an inordinate love of self. In Peer
Gynt egoism takes the form of lust for sensuous pleasure. You will have to go far, I think, to find a more
classic example of pure egoism.

In our present study of Peer Gynt the man, we shall
restrict ourselves to a brief consideration of his conduct
and behavior in each of the five acts that make up the
play. Like all plays built upon the traditional or
Shakespearean model, Peer Gynt is divided into five
parts: 1) introduction or exposition; 2) rising action;
3) climax; 4) falling action; 5) catastrophe. Of these
the introduction takes up a good part of the first act.
Here we learn to know Peer Gynt as he was when he
first faces life "on his own." If we look at him from a

purely objective point of view, he is a wretched spect-
acle. He has wasted some of the best years of his life.
He is twenty years old, but, as his mother complains,
has never done a profitable day's work in all that time.
Yet he demands much of life; demands much of everything and everybody — but not of himself. Of himself
he demands nothing at all. As a result his condition is
somewhat deplorable. Yet it seems to me that I have
seen any number of young people today who show a
remarkable resemblance to the Peer Gynt of Act I.

If, on the other hand, we look at him from a purely
subjective point of view, taking into consideration his
environment and other attendant circumstances, his
condition is not so bad. In fact, we marvel that it is not
worse. He has had a wretched bringing up. "His father was a drunkard and his mother was weak; no wonder he is a good-for-nothing," says Aslak Smith. It
surely is not his fault that he is not a better son than he
is. Fundamentally, he has never done anything evil,
unless we adopt the negative attitude and say that he has
done nothing good. By nature he is kind and amiable;
somewhat wild, somewhat mischievous and unmanage-
able, of course, but no worse than many others. Moreover, he is distinctly gifted in many ways. In spite of
all this he is lacking entirely in the higher ideals of life.
But where should he have acquired any?

Here, then, is Peer Gynt on the threshold of his life
adventure. It begins for him — and with it the rising
action of the play — with the wedding festival at Hegstad. The works of Ibsen are full of crucial situations,
and this is one of them. Here is another "Hercules at
the cross-roads." Wherever Peer turns at the wedding,
he meets those whose only purpose in life seems to be
to lead him astray. But then — suddenly and for the
first time — he meets one who the reader feels intui-
tively is destined to be his redeeming angel. She is a
young girl named Solveig. Her very name attracts our
attention. Solveig is the personification of everything

that is beautiful and good — purity, modesty, innocence.
It is much to Peer's credit that he is impressed, deeply
impressed.

> How fair! Did you ever see the like!
> Looked down at her shoes and her snow-white apron —!
> And then she held on to her mother's skirt folds,
> And carried a hymn book wrapped up in a kerchief —!
> I must look at that girl.

Yes, observe her closely, Peer! For it is she who can
make a man of you — make you "the whole man, the
true, as you were conceived in the mind of God." She
is willing to do it; you too have made an impression on
her. She has even begun to love you. Instinctively she
has sensed what God intended you should be. She sees
you at your best, and sees what possibilities are in you.
You stand at the parting of the ways; you will now be
saved or lost.

Yes, Peer, observe her; observe her closely!

Four times during the wedding festival she crosses his
path. And each time he senses her presence like a ray
from a brighter, purer, higher world. But at the wedding there are other forces working. There is brandy.
There are evil-minded associates of his own age. There
are men and women who egg him on to foolish acts
with their merciless mockery and scorn. And, worse
than all, there is Peer's wild ungovernable nature. What
does Peer do? He attempts to draw Solveig down to
him instead of giving her the opportunity of drawing
him up to her. And when he fails in this, he deserts
her, kidnaps the bride, and flees to the mountains.

Peer Gynt is at the cross-roads. But he does not
make the choice of Hercules. He does not grasp the
hand that is stretched out to give him aid. He turns
from Solveig, in spite of the fact that he sees in her the
most beautiful, the most gracious girl he has ever known
— a revelation from a world that hitherto has been distinctly foreign to him. And in doing all this he is false
to his better self; with both eyes wide open, he deliber-
ately chooses the road that leads to the land of wasted

lives. This is his first great failure, his first great sin.
From a subjective point of view, he leaves the wedding
a different man entirely from the one who came.

Peer has also thrust Solveig from his thoughts. But
"he who has tasted ambrosia from the beakers of the
gods can never be satisfied with ordinary drink." Consequently, Peer can never forget Solveig, even though
he continues to sink lower and lower morally. It is this
gradual ethical degeneration that Ibsen reveals in the
second and third acts by means of symbolism.

Peer soon tires of his stolen bride, the frivolous Ingrid
Hegstad. He cannot help it. Who is she compared
with Solveig?

> Is your hymn-book in your kerchief?
> Hangs the gold-lock o'er your shoulders?
> Do you glance adown your apron?
> Do you hold your mother's skirt fold?
> Went you to the pastor this last spring tide?
> Is there shyness in your glances?
> Does your presence sanctify?
>
> No, but —
>
> What's all the rest then?

And so they part. In the meantime his mother and
Solveig are out in the mountains searching for him. It
seems, therefore, that it would not be difficult for Peer
to return to Solveig. But to him the road already seems
long and difficult. After he has parted from Ingrid, he
seems for a moment ready to leave his old life behind.
In a short soliloquy he says:

> To crush, overturn, stem the rush of the foss!
> To strike! Wrench the fir tree right up by the root!
> This is life. This both hardens and lifts one high!
> To hell then with all the savorless lies.

The mood lasts but a moment. Some sæter-girls' come
upon the scene, and he goes with them. And this time
it is evident to us that he gives in without any inner
struggle. The sæter-girls are on an even lower level

1Girls who in the summer time have charge of the mountain dairies.

than was Ingrid — and as we all know, her plane was low enough. The sæter-girls are still human beings, but they have had intimate relations with trolls; they bridge the gap between men and trolls. They are half trolls.

When Peer deserts the sæter-girls he gives vent to his thoughts in another soliloquy. He seems very much in earnest. He is thoroughly disgusted with himself and makes a number of good resolutions. High above him in the clear, pure mountain air, he sees two brown eagles winging southward. He springs to his feet and cries:

> I'll fly too! I will wash myself clean in
> The bath of the keenest winds!
> I'll fly high! I will purge myself fain in
> The glorious christening font!
> I will soar far over the water,
> I will ride myself-pure of soul.

But his good resolutions again last but a moment. The Green-clad One crosses his path, and he immediately begins making overtures to her. She, however, is none other than the daughter of the Dovre-gnome, the king of the trolls. The Green-clad One, consequently, is an out-and-out troll, and Peer in making advances to her is approaching nearer and nearer "trolldom." But what does the word *troll* signify? It is the symbol of all that is wicked, evil, sinful. That which has to do with *troll* and *trolldom* is the direct antithesis of all that is truly human. The same symbol occurs, not only in Ibsen, but in our folk-literature and in the works of Jonas Lie and Garborg. There is this difference, however; Ibsen uses it as the symbol for that which is the *root* of all evil — namely egoism.

> Among men the saying goes: "Man, be thyself!"
> At home with us 'mid the tribe of the trolls,
> The saying goes: "Troll, to thyself be — enough."

So says the Dovre-gnome. The distinction is clear.

Thus we see Peer going from good to bad, from bad to worse: Solveig to Ingrid; Ingrid to the sæter-girls

who are half trolls; and the sæter-girls to the Green-clad
One who is all troll. The next step is that the Green-
clad One takes him to the hall of the Dovre-gnome,
where she and her tribe plan to transform him into a real
troll. Peer doesn't seem to object at all.

> For a bride, and a well managed kingdom to boot,
> I can put up with losing a good many things.

One thing only he demands — that he be allowed to
return to the world of men should he ever desire to do
so. But in this he is disappointed. The Dovre-gnome
tells him most emphatically that the troll-gate opens in
one direction only — inward. Peer begins to protest.

> I am willing to swear that a cow is a maid,
> An oath one can always eat up again:—
> But to know that one never can free oneself,
> That one can't even die like an honest soul;
> That's a thing I can never agree to.

* * * *

His protests, however, are in vain. The Dovre-gnome
becomes so angry that he gives "big trolls and little
trolls" alike permission to do with Peer as they please.
They treat him most shamefully, but luckily for Peer,
the distant church bells — against whose power the
trolls are impotent — begin to ring and he is saved.

He escapes from the hall of the Dovre-gnome and
tries to return to his own people. But now he meets the
Boyg — "the great Boyg."

People have spent much time on the problem of what
Ibsen has in mind when he created "the great Boyg." If
we consider Peer Gynt merely as an 1860 Norwegian,
the solution is indeed difficult. But if we see him as
the typical human being, the answer is simple. For each
day we, too, meet the Boyg, the voice within us that
whispers, "Go around — take the easiest way." It is
the cold sluggish spirit of inertia which blocks our path
when we are trying to escape from "the hall of the
Mountain King." Always this is true; he is to be found
on the road that leads *away* from evil — the Boyg who

cannot be wounded; the Boyg who is sorely hurt; the Boyg who is dead, the Boyg who is alive; the Boyg who wins without fighting — who merely stands in our way and cries: "Go around — take the easiest way. Why struggle? Why humble yourself? Why deny yourself anything? Go around." Many people call the Boyg the Old Adam, and I know of no better name for him. On the road leading to the Dovre-gnome's hall, Peer finds no Boyg. It is only when he wishes to return.

What happens? Peer gives up the struggle —

> Too dear the purchase one pays for life
> In such a heart wasting hour of strife.

He sinks to earth. At this moment, however, Aase and Solveig again set the church bells ringing, and Peer escapes a second time from the forces of evil. But for him the escape is no moral victory. It is merely a stroke of good luck of the type pictured in fairy tales. Peer himself has done nothing at all to redeem himself; he is no different from what he was before meeting "the great Boyg." Yet there is still hope. He has not forgotten Solveig. "Tell her not to forget me," he admonishes her younger sister Helga. With this speech the second act closes.

In the beginning of the third act, Ibsen allows us glimpses of a number of highly significant incidents. First we see Peer, deep in a pine forest, cutting timber for the cabin he is building for himself. He is alone, for he had been outlawed after the bride-rape at Hegstad. Working thus in the forest, Peer comes upon a youth, who, to escape service in the king's army, chops off one of his fingers with a sickle. This young man has decided that if he is to continue supporting his mother, his wife, and his child, he *must* resort to this expedient. And he does it. To Peer, such resolution, such courage, such forgetfulness of self and such regard for others is entirely incomprehensible.

> An unmendable finger
> Right off! And with no one compelling him to it.
> Ay, think of it, wish it done — will it to boot, —
> But do it —! No that's past my understanding.

Of course it is! Had you comprehended it, Peer, we might have escaped the next scene Ibsen shows us. Here we see what is happening at the old homestead. Everything has been sold, farm and all, except the poor cottage where Aase is permitted to stay as long as she lives. But it will not be long. She is sick already and must take to her bed. This is what Peer has done for his mother. Life is never so empty, so fruitless, both for us and for others as when we think only of ourselves.

Even now Solveig has not forgotten Peer. Once more she extends a willing hand. The poor outlaw will certainly not refuse the proffered aid now. Surely he will accept it, no matter what the effort may cost him.

Peer has just finished building his cabin and is busily engaged in making its doors secure against all comers. He will even bar out the "hobgoblin thoughts" that come to plague him. And we can scarcely blame him for that. They can be most exasperating, these malicious spirits, especially for one who has lived like Peer.

But what is this? Can it be possible? Yes, it is true! Solveig comes! And to me what she says to Peer is the most beautiful speech in the whole drama.

> One message you sent me by little Helga;
> Others came after in storm and in stillness.
> All that your mother told bore me a message,
> That brought forth others when dreams sank upon me.
> Nights full of heaviness, blank empty days,
> Brought me the message that now I must come.
> It seemed as though life had been quenched down there;
> I could not laugh nor weep from the depths of my heart.
> I knew not for sure how you might be minded;
> I knew but for sure what I should do and must do.

Peer can scarcely believe his ears:

> Oh, who would have thought I could draw you to me, —
> Ah, but I have longed for you, daylong and nightlong.

But is it possible that Solveig is willing to become his wife? Solveig! Will she not soon regret what she has done and then leave him? But Solveig answers:

> The path I have trodden leads back nevermore.

Now for the first time we find Peer willing to forget himself for others. For Solveig he will tear down the little cabin and rebuild it for her.

> Warm shall the fire be and bright shall it shine,
> You shall sit softly and never be a-cold.

His egoism continues to wane. He is on the verge of becoming a new man. His redeeming angel has again crossed his pathway.

But Peer can never become a new man without a struggle — that is self evident. Consequently we wonder how he will fare when he again encounters the Boyg. We do not have to wait long. The Boyg is not far distant.

This time it is the Green-clad One who assumes the role. When Peer steps into the forest for a moment, leaving Solveig alone in the cabin, the Green-clad One accosts him and demands a share in his life. She tells him he will never be rid of her, whether he marries Solveig or not.

Of course the speech is figurative, but the meaning is clear. It is his past life with all its nastiness which persists in dogging him. And Peer realizes that he must struggle, sacrifice, forget himself completely, if he is to become worthy of Solveig, to lift himself to her level. It is the very self-negation which he has always feared.

Repentance? And maybe 'twould take whole years
Ere I fought my way through. 'Twere a meagre life, that,
To shatter what's radiant, and lovely, and pure,
And clench it together in fragments and shards?
You can do it with a fiddle, but not with a bell.
Go in after this? So befouled and disgraced? —
Go in with that troll-rabble after me still?
Speak, yet be silent; confess, yet conceal —?
No! — I must roundabout then — as best I may.

And so Peer turns aside — takes the easiest way. He
deserts Solveig; gives her up without a blow. Solveig,
who had sacrificed everything in life for him.

Thus Peer chooses, this time for life. For this is his
critical choice, his last chance to redeem himself. It is
also the climax of the play, the high point in the rising
action. Of course there is still one who has a moral
right to be dependent on him: his old, sick mother. But
as we have learned to expect by this time, Peer is soon
rid of her. Then he goes out into the world, determined
to live his own life, to live for Peer and for Peer only.

In the fourth act, the falling action begins. The time
is about thirty years later. We find Peer, together with
a number of friends for whom he is giving a dinner
party, in a palm grove on the coast of Morocco. He is
now exactly what we had looked for — an out and out
pleasure-loving egoist.

Drink, gentlemen! If man is made
For pleasure, let him take his fill then.

are the first words he speaks in Act IV. He has been
living in America and has done exceedingly well. He
is rich. As for the rest, he gives an excellent portrait of
himself in the following words:

If you could but see my innermost self
You'd find only Peer there, and Peer all through, —
Nothing else in the world, no, nor anything more.

And Peer is demanding nothing small.

But I must be myself — en bloc,
Must be the Gynt of all the planet.

He merely wants the whole world.

In the dinner party scene, and especially in the caricature of the astounding prayer which Peer offers when his faithless friends run off with his yacht and his money, it has been Ibsen's task to show Peer to us as a most "far gone" egoist, and I know of no author who has performed his task so well. In the remainder of the fourth act, which in one sense is a complete drama in itself, Peer's absolute lack of character is always in the foreground. The egoism of the pleasure seeker and his lack of character go hand in hand.

In this little drama there are also five acts: that is, five scenes in which Peer takes the leading roles — each role being more absurd, more idiotic than the preceding. In the first scene he plans to make the Sahara desert a huge irrigation project, and this new land, flowing with milk and honey shall be called *Gyntiana* and its capital *Peeropolis*. In the next scene he becomes the prophet of a tribe of Arabs. But when he discovers that with prophets also "familiarity breeds contempt", he runs away with Anitra, an Arab girl, convinced that the fountain of all true living is love and eternal youth. This is the height of absurdity, and the climax of the little drama. But Peer is disappointed in his dream of love and youth eternal. Anitra deserts him, and he becomes a philosopher ready to solve the riddle of the Sphinx. The last scene shows Peer an emperor, but emperor of the poor lunatics in an insane asylum in Cairo. The most noticeable feature of the fourth act is that Peer never chooses the roles he plays — he assumes them without being at all conscious of the fact.

But Ibsen is not through with Peer. There are yet some traits of egoism to be portrayed. He wants to show us that just as truly as Peer is to himself everything, others are to him absolutely nothing. This is the theme in Act V.

Here we meet Peer on board a ship which is nearing the coast of Norway. A storm is brewing and Peer fears

for his life. To make his peace with God, should anything happen, he tells the captain:

> If any of your crew are in real need,
> I won't look too closely after the money.

The captain thanks him, saying that it is very kind of
him:

> That's kind. They are most of them ill enough off;
> They have all got their wives and their children at home.
> With their wages alone they can scarcely make ends meet;
> But if they come home with some cash to the good,
> It will be a return not forgot in a hurry.

This is an idea Peer had never once thought of. He is
not at all eager to make the crew happy. His only
thought is to get into the good graces of the Lord, so
that he may weather the storm in safety.

> They are married? They have someone at home who cares,
> Who is glad in their coming? But me!
> There is never a soul who gives me a thought!
> Are there lights in the windows? Those lights shall be darkened!
> I'll get even with them! Not a soul shall be sober,
> I'll send them home drunk to their wives and their children.

There we have it. It is Peer all over again. Such is the
inordinate love of self. But the scenes are shifting, and
the catastrophe is at hand. Now for the first time Peer
must come face to face with his past life. We are sorry
for Peer. His task will be a difficult one. Deeds done
and deeds left undone rise to accuse him. There are
twelve of them — and all denounce him. In this jury
there is unanimity. There is but one verdict: Peer is
guilty.

The first accuser is the Strange Passenger, who, without Peer's having caught a glimpse of him, has been on
board ship all the way from Panama. Now, just when
disaster seems imminent, he makes his appearance and
begins speaking mysterious words of "the torch that
guides men on their night-pilgrimages through life" and
of the "multitudes whose ashes rest in urns" — that is,
all the golden opportunities that have been wasted and

the marvelous talents that have remained unused; and concludes by asking so many embarrassing personal questions that Peer finds him most ungracious and inquisitive. When he finally goes his way, Peer desides that he was just a "sorry moralist", nothing more. To us, however, the Strange Passenger represents Peer's awakening conscience, his fear of seeing himself as he is or as he has been. I know very well that Ibsen in one of his peevish moments, declared that the Strange Passenger had no particular significance. Be that as it may, he plays a most significant role, whether Ibsen was conscious of the fact or not.

The second accuser is a minister preaching the funeral sermon of a man, who, when summoned for military service, chopped off one of his fingers that he might remain at home to support his mother, his wife, and his child. The minister has only praise for this man who used his little talent as best he knew. He had, the minister declared, "been himself." And Peer, listening, knows very well that this praise is for the youth he encountered in the forest years before. A man whose life has differed more widely from that of Peer can scarcely be imagined. Yet Peer, at the end of the sermon, concludes that the same words could be spoken over *his* coffin. He too has "been himself."

The third accuser is the auction at his old homestead. Everything is being sold. Peer himself is remembered only as "an abominable liar" who long since was hanged over in America. The fourth is a wild onion with many layers but no center — an admirable representation of himself, it seems to Peer. He is now beginning to realize that the matter is serious. And this feeling grows when he meets the fifth accuser — a cabin which seems strangely familiar. There is a woman inside the cabin who sings of one who promised to return, and for whom she will wait. It is Solveig who sings. Quietly and with face blanched, Peer springs to his feet.

One that's remembered — and one that's forgot.
One that has squandered — and one that has saved. —
Oh, earnest! — and never can the game be played o'er!
Oh, dread — here was my Kaiserdom.

But more than this, even, is needed before Peer will
realize that "the wheel is come full circle." Instead of
revealing himself to the faithful Solveig who has awaited
his coming for thirty years, he turns and hurries away.
Soon he reaches a heath where a forest fire has been raging. As he picks his way among the charred tree trunks,
this blasted heath becomes his next accuser. Another
representation of my life, thinks Peer. And from now
on he meets with reproach in all he sees and hears. Balls
of gray yarn rolling at his feet declare that they are the
thoughts he has refused to think. Withered leaves flying
before the wind whisper that they are the ideals he has
failed to realize; and soughings in the wind itself mur-
mur that they are the songs he has never sung. Nor is
this all. Drops of dew as they fall from the trees bring to
memory the tears unshed, and broken straws the work
undone. Finally he hears his mother's voice complain-
ing that he has directed her to the wrong place. Thus it
goes. In all there are twelve indictments against him,
only one of which accuses him of an offense which he
has actually committed. All the others reproach him for
neglecting to do what he should have done.

Finally the judge appears. He is the Button Moulder.
And his judgment is this: Because you have made a
mess of your life, you must go into the melting pot with
others of your kind, and be recast.

Now you were designed for a shining button
On the vest of the world, but your loop gave way;
So into the waste box you needs must go,
And then as the phrase is, be merged in the mass.

Peer, however, begins to protest. Most emphatically he
declares: "Anything but that." He refused to be
merged in the mass, to lose one doit of his "Self."
Rather than subject himself to the merging process, he

will endure the torments of hell. The Button Moulder agrees that this is a possible alternative, provided of course, that he can prove himself a genuine sinner. "No lukewarm sinner, or one just so-so" will ever do. Peer's mind is made up immediately. He will take the way of perdition — and off he runs in search of someone who will affirm that he has been sinful enough to qualify. But to find such a person is not so easy as it appears. His record is made up of sins of omission, not sins of commission. His greatest sin is that he has done nothing. His talents have been allowed to lie idle. He is a bungler, a fool, and nothing remains for him but the melting pot.

> But for one who like you has smudged himself out,
> Neither sulphur nor potash avails in the least.

Peer is in a quandary. There are but these two alternatives, the melting ladle and the way of perdition. He refuses to go into the one, and he cannot get into the other. Later a third way will present itself — the kingdom of God, the way of salvation. But for the present there can be no thought of salvation — at least for Peer. He doesn't even desire it.

No — he *must* find someone who will furnish proof that he is a sinner. And finally he is successful. He comes once more to the cabin of Solveig. She certainly knows him for what he is. Triumphantly he turns to the Button Moulder, who has again reminded him to put his house in order:

> Set my house in order? It's true! Away!
> Get you gone! Though your ladle were huge as a coffin,
> It were too small, I tell you, for me and my sins.

But the Boyg is not yet dead. For one brief moment there is danger that Peer will attempt to avoid the issue, to "go around." *Peer* (approaches the hut)

Forward and back, and it's just as far.
Out and in, and it's just as strait.
No! — like a wild, an unending lament,
Is the thought: to come back, to go in, to go home.
(Takes a few steps on, but stops again)
Round about, said the Boyg!
(Hears singing in the hut)
Ah no; *this time at least*
Right through, though the way be never so strait!

Just then Solveig appears in the doorway, dressed for
church, her hymn book wrapped in her kerchief. She
stands there kind, erect. Peer throws himself down on
the threshold.

Hast thou doom for a sinner, then speak it forth!
Cry out all my sins and my trespasses!

But Solveig has no indictment to bring against him:

In nothing have you sinned, my own dear boy.
* * * *
Blessed be thou that at last thou hast come.

Now Peer is actually terrified and cries out wildly: "I
am lost!" He is still convinced that the melting ladle
and the way of perdition are the only alternatives. And
if in the eyes of Solveig he is no sinner, then hope is
gone. He is doomed to the melting ladle. But Solveig
knows better. With quiet good nature she makes
reply:

There is one that rules all things.

But Peer laughs.

Lost! Unless you can answer riddles.
Solveig: Tell me them.
Peer: Tell them! Come on! To be sure!
Canst thou tell where Peer Gynt has been since we parted?
With his destiny's seal on his brow;
Been, as in God's thought he first sprang forth!
Canst thou tell me? If not, I must get me home, —
Go down to the mist shrouded regions.
Solveig (Smiling): Oh, that riddle is easy.
Peer: Then tell what thou knowest!
Where was I, as myself, as the whole man, the true man?
Where was I, with God's sigil upon my brow?

Solveig: In my faith, in my hope, and in my love.
Peer: What sayest thou — ? Peace! These are juggling words.
           Thou art mother thyself to the man that's there.

He means that to "the man that's there" — to the one
who has existed in her faith, her hope, and her love —
she herself has been the mother; but that this man has
never existed except in her love. To this statement Solveig answers:

> Ay, that I am; but who is his father?
> Surely he that forgives at the mother's prayer.

That is to say: Yes, I *am* mother to this man. But his
true self has given me his likenes. You have lived in
my love, in my heart, not as you actually have lived
since we parted but as I saw you at our first meeting —
the embodiment of what God intended you should be.
It is the man with God's seal on his brow who has lived
in my heart. And he, who at our first meeting, permitted me to see you as you were conceived in the
mind of God, will, at my prayer, forgive you for not
living according to his plan; will forgive you for
hitherto defying your true life's destiny.

Now a "gleam of light" flashes across Peer's face, and
he cries out:

> My mother; my wife; oh thou innocent woman! —
> In thy love — oh, there hide me, hide me.
>
> (He clings to her and hides his face in her lap.
> A long silence. The sun rises.)

And thus finally Peer is saved. The sun rises.

Solveig has taught him two things. In the first
place, she has convinced him that both his creator, with
whom he has broken faith throughout his whole life,
and Solveig, whom of all people he has treated most
shamefully, have forgiven him. It follows as a matter
of course that both the melting ladle and the way of perdition forfeit their rights to him. They have nothing
more to say. And in the second place she has taught

him the meaning of true affection; she has taught him
to love. As Brand says to Agnes:

> No single soul can all contain
> Except it first have yearn'd for one.

At this moment it is psychologically needful for Peer
to love Solveig — truly love her. But at the same moment that love finds a place in his heart, egoism
vanishes, and Peer is a new man.

Thus in the end Solveig becomes his redeeming
angel in that she teaches him faith, hope, and love.
She cannot restore his wasted life — all his opportunities for doing good. But she has redeemed *him* and the
remainder of his life. The sun is finally shining upon
Peer. Finally! It was his own fault that it is the set-
ting, not the rising sun.

The PRETENDERS
Translated by NILS FLATEN

THE PRETENDERS

INTRODUCTION

A. THE PRETENDERS IN HISTORY

I

The Pretenders as a Historical Drama.

The Pretenders is first and foremost what we may call a psychological or character drama. When Ibsen wrote *The Pretenders*, it was not his main purpose or aim to present a portion of the history of Norway, nor to set before us a lifelike picture of Haakon Haakonsson, Skule Baardsson, Bishop Nikolas, and many other personages whom he describes. But he has done both these things, and with a mastery so great that his historical dramas — and not least *The Pretenders* — have become epoch making in this field. Reading *The Pretenders* we seem to be reading one of the best sagas, so genuine and natural, so true in their resemblance to the sagas are the spirit and force of the whole drama.

Not only are we brought into contact with the mode of thought and life of that period, becoming as it were participants of all the fights and tumults in which that epoch was so rich, and compelled to take sides for or against the personages involved; but the author has been able to make these persons' language and style so surpassingly similar to those of the sagas, that we almost forget that *The Pretenders* is written in the middle of the 19th century and that the language is Norwegian-Danish.

No doubt Ibsen has been free in his treatment of historical facts. With regard to personalities, the majority of them have in Ibsen's hands been made to appear considerably greater than they were in reality. Haakon Haakonsson, for example, has become so great that all

the rest appear like dwarfs beside him. This is of course
exaggeration. And it is not probable that he possessed
that surpassingly clear and rational insight, especially
with regard to the demands of his times, with which Ibsen has endowed him. It is perhaps Ibsen who also has
lent him the great *king's-thought.*

And Skule was not according to the sagas such a complete incarnation of doubt and misgivings and — we
may add — respect for right as Ibsen has made him.
In like manner Jatgeir Skald and, most of all, perhaps,
the women in *The Pretenders,* have been highly idealized.
Bishop Nikolas has been made to serve as the model
of one of the most devilish men that the hand of a poet
has ever drawn. It is probable that Bishop Nikolas was
not quite so bad. — And Ibsen has been quite free in his
treatment of historical facts. According to need, he has
modified or added, and combined several events, which
chronologically may be separated by several years. As,
for example, the ordeal (1218) and the election of king
(1223).

But, in spite of this arbitrary handling of his material,
he has succeeded, as already mentioned, in creating a
historical drama more faithful to the spirit and color of
the sagas than any poet had been able to do before him.
"It is in the conception and representation of Northern
antiquity that Ibsen — and later Bjørnson — set a
landmark in the history of literature." (Henrik Jæger.)

And when Ibsen has occasion to handle historical material in this fashion, he knows well how to adapt it to
his use: To present his own ideas and experiences.
The history of the period concerned (1st half of the 13th
century) thus adapted, may thus be said to have served
merely as a springboard from which he leaped over into
his own epoch and his own intellectual world. He has
used the most outstanding personages in *The Pretenders*
as types or personifications of this or that idea of which

he felt the urge to give a clear and intelligible expression (See below, pp. 82ff.).

Thus, *The Pretenders* might perhaps with some profit be read merely as psychological drama, without regard to the historical element. But it will appear from what has already been said, that one might also with some profit read *The Pretenders* merely as a historical drama. For, as already indicated, he has not given us a caricature of either the persons or the period involved. In their main characteristics the personages were as he has described them; he has only made them greater, finer, more important, more beautiful — or more hideous — than they were. And the period as a whole is treated in like manner. He has given us a true and adequate picture of the conditions of that time, however much he may have treated the various events in accordance with his own judgment. But even the contributions of his own making might have been true. They fit the times.

With all this in mind it will be easy to understand that the full benefit of the study of *The Pretenders* will be derived only from studying it both as a historical and psychological drama.

The study of *The Pretenders* as a historical drama presupposes naturally some knowledge of the history of Norway. We need especially to apprehend one side of it, namely, the character and history of the Norwegian monarchy. In the first place, because the history of the monarchy is, so to speak, the center of the history of the entire saga period. It stands as the central point of the nation's intellectual and political life. Throughout the middle ages (the period of the sagas) and the modern epoch the history of the monarchy and that of the nation are identical in important points. "A decline of the monarchy meant dissolution and weakness of the state itself, advancement of the monarchy brought honor and greatness to the whole nation." (Oscar Albert Johnson.)

II

THE NORWEGIAN MONARCHY

1. The Norwegian Monarchy before Harald Haarfagre.

The ancient petty kings and regional chieftains had little power and authority. The king in his relations to the other chieftains within his domain was rather to be considered as the first among equals *(primus inter pares).* Above all he was the chief commander of his territory in times of war. In some districts he might combine therewith the functions of the priesthood. But the title of king often gave him a prestige and dignity of far greater import than his formal power and authority.

The title of king was inherited, and all his sons had an equal right to the throne. The kingdom was held by allodial rights, in private ownership, and pertained to the family who at one time had gained possession of it. The king and the royal domain stood in the same relationship as an allodial proprietor and his estate. The ownership was absolute, but the land must go in succession to the sons, and each son had the same right of inheritance. If the king had several sons, the *fylkesting,* or assembly, decided which one should have the preference, and there was no discrimination made between those of legitimate and illegitimate birth.

2. Harald Haarfagre unites Norway into one Kingdom.

Then came Harald Haarfagre, and the 31 *Fylker,* or petty kingdoms, into which Norway up to that time had been divided, were by him combined into one kingdom. He creates the kingdom of Norway, forming the third kingdom of northern Europe, Sweden and Denmark having already long ago attained national unity.

This was something new to Norway and of course a violent infringement on what before had been considered right and fitting. When Harald made himself sole king, he took away the royal authority from each of the 31 petty kings, who up to that time had possessed it —

each in his small domain. These kings must now submit to the alternative of either becoming Harald's vassals or leave the country. But Harald not only made himself sole king, but also absolute monarch. He assumed all power of arbitrary rule.

It goes without saying that this was a severe blow to the many refractory chieftains, who until then had been accustomed to yield to no authority, except such as they themselves had agreed to establish. They especially found it intolerable that Harald assumed the right of taxing the land. A tax on allodial estates was something unheard of. It was more than many of them would submit to. They would not be the king's tenants. Rather would they abandon the country and seek new homes in foreign lands. And many did so — especially from the three southwest *Fylker*, or districts, which at that time were the foremost both in outward might and in culture: Hordaland, Rogaland, and Agder. But except in these three *Fylker*, most of the chieftains remained. Harald once for all was king, — it is true, only by right of the strongest; but this right meant much in those days; victory was accepted as a divine judgment by which one must abide. But the period from now until the battle of Stiklestad (1030) witnessed a continual struggle between the Norwegian monarchy and the Norwegian aristocracy, and this is, more than anything else, the outstanding feature of the Norwegian history of this period.

The Norwegian monarchy as founded by Harald Haarfagre was based first of all upon two claims: Norway was to be one realm, and it must be hereditary in the family of Harald Haarfagre. But these two principles were necessarily accompanied by a third and very important one: Norway must be independent; for neither unity nor inheritance can be maintained without independence. And to assert now one, then the other, and often all three of these principles at once, the Norwegian monarchy is compelled to carry on a long, hard fight with the aristocracy.

Harald succeeded in maintaining all three principles. It would seem that he renounced the one for which he had fought the hardest, that of unity. The saga tells that at the age of 70, that is in 920, he summoned his many and unruly sons to a meeting in Oplandene, there giving to each of them — legitimate and illegitimate — the royal title and a share in the kingdom, himself remaining over-king and stipulating that his favorite son, Erik Bloodaxe, should be his successor. Thus there were again several kings in Norway; but this was unavoidable because of the principle of inheritance, a principle so firmly rooted that it undoubtedly never occurred to Harald or any one else that a change was possible. But the matter of over-king was something new, invented by him just to preserve the unity of the country.

We can now easily understand how this establishment of many subject kings and one over-king easily might become a source of endless and bitter strife, and this was precisely what happened, as we shall point out below. All things considered, Harald was not to blame. He, in fact, took the only course possible, if he were to preserve the unity of the kingdom and at the same time assert the ancient rule of inheritance.

3. The Norwegian Monarchy from Erik Bloodaxe (930) to the Battle of Stiklestad (1030).

Harald found it relatively easy both to assert himself against the aristocrats and, during the last ten years of his reign, to maintain his position as his sons' overlord. But what was easy for Harald to accomplish by dint of his powerful personality, ability to govern, and liberality, became impossible for his son Erik. In military ability Erik was perhaps his father's equal, but as a king and ruler he was inefficient. Besides, he was harsh and cruel, and allowed himself to be led by his beautiful but wicked queen, Gunhild, who was much worse than he. His brothers reluctantly submitted to his rule, wherupon Erik killed several of them, while Gunhild egged him on to slay them all. He also offended many of the other great men of the country.

It is therefore not surprising that discontent grew, and that the aristocrats seized the first opportunity for reaction. Harald's youngest son, Haakon, who had been brought up in England, at the court of King Adelstein, and is therefore known as Adelsteinsfostre, was made to come home, and Sigurd Ladejarl, who perhaps was at that time the most powerful of all the Norwegian chieftains, argued his case so well that he without difficulty was proclaimed king, first at Nidaros, later in other parts of the country. Erik and Gunhild, together with their eight sons, were driven from the country.

Thus Haakon mounted the throne by the help of the nobles. It was therefore natural that they would see to it that Haakon did not obtain the same authority as his father had assumed. It is true that he received more and greater prerogatives than the former petty kings had possessed, but these prerogatives the nobles had voluntarily agreed to. First of all Haakon had to renounce the right of arbitrarily taxing the land. "He restored to the landowners their allodial rights (odel)," says the saga. Taxes he did receive, but only by agreement with the nobles. Thus ended the absolute power of the king. But what the monarchy lost in power it regained in that it from now on struck deeper roots in the nation's appreciation and favor.

Haakon ruled many years, and ruled well, whence he was named Haakon the Good. But the Erikssons, or Gunhildssons, as they were often called, started a movement to make away with Haakon and thus get possession of their inheritance, receiving help from the Danish king. Haakon easily held his own in two battles. The third and last battle was fought on the island of Stord, and here Haakon was slain (961). Before his death he gave all Norway to those of the Gunhildssons who were yet alive, and Harald Graafeld, the oldest, was to be the over-king. Harald Graafeld and his brothers now became kings in Norway, but under the Danish king's suzerainty, this being his reward for aiding them against Haakon. The independence of Norway was therefore sacrificed.

Gunhild became virtually the ruler, and her sons and their government soon became hated everywhere. When they were unwise enough to attack the powerful Sigurd Ladejarl and burn him and his men in the house where they were gathered, his son, the later famous Haakon Ladejarl, fled to Denmark, inducing the Danish king, Harald Blaatand, to invite Harald Graafeld down to Denmark, where he was murdered. Gunhild and her two surviving sons were banished the second time.

The Danish king and Haakon then proceeded to Norway, meeting with little or no opposition. They divided the country between them, and the Danish king ruled through subject kings, these as well as Haakon paying tribute to the Danes. And now the work of Harald Haarfagre was seriously imperilled. Norway was under Danish suzerainty, disunited, and Harald Haarfagre's dynasty was out. In fact, the political situation was as before the consolidation under Harald.

When Haakon Jarl had defeated the Jomsvikings at Hjorungavaag (986), he ruled over his part of the country as an independent monarch until 995. But then Olav Tryggvesson comes to the fore, — the man who has the honor of having restored the Norwegian kingdom, and not only restored, but strengthened it. Above all others of whom the sagas give account Olav is to the Norwegians the ideal of a man; and by his brilliant personality he gives new lustre to the kingdom. As the first leader of the movement to introduce Christianity he made the monarchy a representative of Christianity. And this was a matter of great significance. The kingdom had from the very beginning been democratic, representing the whole people over against the aristocracy. From now on it became also the representative of a new invincible spiritual power over against the old, effete, and decadent paganism. He thus gave the monarchy a new spiritual basis. — Olav Tryggvesson was strong, and he used the "right of the strongest" to a greater extent than any king preceding him since Harald Haarfagre. He also exercised much cruelty in introducing Christianity. But in these days the people would endure most anything at the hands of a man like Olav Tryggvesson. In spite of everything there has probably never in Norway been a king so highly popular as Olav Tryggvesson. And when he fell in the battle of Svolder (1000), there was mourning throughout the land.

The victors at Svolder, the Swedish and Danish kings, and Erik Jarl, the son of Haakon Jarl, now divided Norway among them. And while the two foreign kings allowed their parts to be governed by Erik and his brother Svein, yet, the work of Harald Haarfagre seemed to be a thing of the past.

Then, in 1015 appears again a descendant of Harald Haarfagre in the person of Olav Haraldsson. And it soon became evident how firmly rooted in the minds of the Norwegian people were the three principles for which Harald Haarfagre had fought. Within less than a year Olav was practically king of all Norway. The Norwegian kingdom was restored and the principles it stood for were clearly set forth in Olav's time. During the whole period of his reign Olav had practically only these two items on his program: everybody, great or small, must obey the law; and everybody must accept Christianity, both privately and publicly. But nothing could be more distasteful to the privileged classes than such restriction of what they considered personal freedom. They hated Olav, and the most powerful chieftains went over to the Danish-English king, Knut the Great. The result was the battle of Stiklestad.

4. From the Battle of Stiklestad (1030) to the Death of Sigurd Jorsalfar (1130).

With the battle of Stiklestad we reach the climax or turning point in the history of the saga period. The battle of Stiklestad is at the same time the most tragic defeat and the most glorious victory known to the sagas. By his defeat and death Olav gained victory for his cause. Even before the battle we perceive that the leaders of the hostile forces had a faint sensation that they fought against a good man and a just cause. For none of them wanted the chief command in the battle. And their victory seems only to have strengthened and clarified this feeling. And when Knut — in direct opposition to his promises to the Norwegian barons — installed his son Svein as king, and the latter ruled unwisely, — as it seemed, aiming directly at offending the Norwegians, this feeling grew rapidly in the minds of all. the result being that within a year Olav was regarded as a saint. Thus in reality Olav's cause was held to be God's cause; and thereby its victory was assured. Christianity prevailed over paganism, and the monarchy over the aristocracy.

Svein was driven from the country in 1035 and Magnus the Good placed on the throne. But Magnus the Good was St. Olav's son, and thus by his accession the kingdom reverted to the family of Harald Haarfagre. The succeeding kings were all of the same lineage until in 1319, when none were left of the direct line. His reign marks also the end of the aristocracy's contention against the monarchy. Not against, but through, the will of the king may the barons hereafter hope again to gain power and influence.

In so far as there were internal disturbances during the next hundred years (1035-1130), they occurred not between king and barons, but between kings who reigned simultaneously. Thus, there was friction between Magnus the Good and his uncle, Harald Haardraade; likewise between Magnus Barefoot and his cousin, Haakon Magnusson. Conditions were even worse during the reigns of Magnus Barefoot's sons, Øistein and Sigurd Jorsalfar, but Øistein's noble character and love of peace prevented actual warfare.

5. *From the Death of Sigurd Jorsalfar (1130) to the Coming of Sverre (1177).*

At the death of Sigurd Jorsalfar begins that long period in Norse history known as the "Civil Wars," the last scene of which is the death of Skule Baardsson (1240). This time too the aristocrats are at the bottom of the trouble, and how the mischief came about we shall try to explain.

Sigurd Jorsalfar had only one son, Magnus, and no other royal princes were known to exist. But shortly before Sigurd's death a young man came from Ireland to Norway; his name was Harald Gille. He claimed to be the son of Magnus Barefoot and an Irish woman, proving his right by the ordeal, and Sigurd recognized him as his brother, but made him promise that he would not assume the royal title as long as he (Sigurd) or his son, Magnus, were living. But no sooner was Sigurd dead and Magnus seated on the throne, when a group of the barons insisted that Harald, too, should be named king. And now begins the struggle with the aristocrats *(lendermenn)*.

But what is the difference between these feudatory lords *(lendermenn)* and the ancient chieftains? A *lendermann* is a man who has received his land holdings from the king on the condition that he is to render certain service to the king: collect the taxes in his district, in war time furnish the king a certain number of men, etc. It was Harald Haarfagre who devised this arrangement. When he had won all Norway he made as many as possible of the old regional chieftains and petty kings his feudal vassals *(lendermenn)*, that is, they became royal functionaries. But these feudal lords would rather be what they had been previously: independent peasant chieftains. They wanted to rule themselves, and therefore they often came into conflict with the king's authority. This was the old aristocratic domination which had come to an end after the battle of Stiklestad. But after the death of Sigurd Jorsalfar it was precisely as the king's *lendermenn*, as his underlings, that they sought to recover their former authority. The weaker the king, the more he needed the help of his vassals, the greater would be their power. Again, if several kings fought for power amongst themselves, it concerned each of these to line up on his side as many *lendermenn* as possible, and the latter usually espoused the cause of the king who would give them the most power and influence.

Harald Gille was weak and yielded to the advice of his men. Hence the majority of the *lendermenn* flocked to him. But his reign nevertheless was short. After a few years Magnus was made captive by Harald, then deposed and blinded (whence he is called Magnus the Blind). But now appears on the scene Sigurd Slembe, a hitherto unknown son of Magnus Barefoot. Sigurd was a man highly gifted, both intellectually and physically, and accordingly the barons opposed with all their might his recognition as a royal prince. Harald Gille was slain by Sigurd Slembe (1136). But Harald left three sons, all children between the ages of two and six, and the barons almost to a man rallied round these boy kings. Then Sigurd Slembe joined forces with Magnus the Blind, who after his downfall had lived as a monk in the monastery at Nidaros; but in the battle of Holmengraa, in the fall of 1139, the barons succeeded in ridding themselves of both these opponents.

As the guardian of these three boy kings, Øistein, Sigurd Mund, and Inge Krokryg, the barons were able to deal with them as they liked; when the kings became

of age they began to quarrel among themselves, and
again it appears that the weakest has the largest number of barons on his side.   This was Inge, weak-minded
and crippled, and among the many chieftains who rallied round him was the capable and powerful Erling
Skakke from Søndhordland (S. W. part of Norway).
In 1155 Sigurd is slain in battle, and Øistein in 1157;
but the barons who had been their partisans would not
transfer their allegiance to Inge.   They propose as their
candidate for the throne Haakon Herdebred, the son of
Sigurd Mund.   The conflict continues until 1161, when
Inge is slain.

The question now arises whether Inge's men will join
Haakon Herdebred.   But they refuse; they would
rather give their allegiance to one who is not of royal
birth.   Erling Skakke's wife was Kristina, the daughter
of Sigurd Jorsalfar; their son was Magnus, now five
years old.   He is of royal descent, but not of the male
line, hence can not claim the throne by right of inheritance.   In spite thereof he was proclaimed king by all
of Inge's party.   The next year Haakon Herdebred was
defeated and slain.   Shortly after the same fate befell
another son of Sigurd Mund, — Sigurd Markusfostre,
whom his followers had named in opposition to Magnus Erlingsson.   But though Erling now had gotten rid
of all his son's rivals, he still realized the deficiency in
that his son was not by birth entitled to the throne.   In
order to overcome this hindrance he sought the support
of the church.   At a national assembly in Bergen, 1163,
he succeeded in having both prelates and barons agree
to a new law of succession to the throne, according to
which the kingdom should be indivisible; the king's
oldest legitimate son should inherit the whole kingdom,
unless "iniquity and incapacity" made him unfit.   In
that case the nearest relative, born in wedlock, even of
the female line, should have the right of succession.
But in any event a select body of prelates and barons,
headed by the archbishop, should decide whether the

one entitled to inherit was worthy of bearing the crown. Norway thus became in reality an elective kingdom, and the right of choosing the king came into the hands of the aristocrats, especially the prelates. And secretly Magnus even took the country for himself and his successors as a fief under St. Olav, "Norway's eternal king." Thereupon Magnus was anointed and crowned by the archbishop, which was also something new in Norway.

From now until 1177 Magnus Erlingsson remained in undisturbed possession of the royal power. It is true that now and then uprisings occurred; but they were all put down without much difficulty by Erling. The last to be quelled was that of the Birchlegs, a band of low-born and poor, but brave and hardy men who had proclaimed as king Øistein Møila, a son of Øistein Haraldsson. At the battle of Re Øistein and a large number of his followers were slain, the remainder saving themselves by flight. The name of Birchlegs had hitherto been a nickname; they were poor and had gotten this name from being compelled to tie birch bark around their feet for want of shoes. But soon a leader was to appear who would make it an honor to be a Birchleg. This leader was Sverre.

6. From Sverre's Appearance (1177) to the Death of Inge Baardsson (1217).

Sverre Sigurdsson was reared by the Bishop of the Faroe Islands and was educated for the priesthood. But then his mother informed him that he was the son of Sigurd Mund, and from that time it became his aim to "overthrow the constitution of 1163, crush the domination of the barons, and bring the country back to the old monarchical course traced by St. Olav."

He arrives in Norway in 1177, finds general satisfaction with Magnus Erlingson and his government. In despondence he goes on a visit to his sister, Cecilia, in Vermland. There he meets the few still surviving

Birchlegs, about 70 in number, poorly clad, without weapons, some of them ill. They forced Sverre to be their leader and proceed along the frontier through what are now the Swedish provinces of Dalarne and Jemteland, many joining them as they advance. They reach Nidaros, and he is proclaimed king at the Øreting. But learning that Erling and Magnus are approaching, he and his Birchlegs seek safety in flight, and for the next two years he is pursued throughout the country like a wild beast. But he does not give up. The number of his Birchlegs increases gradually and Sverre knows how to make them into good soldiers. He finally ventures to meet Erling and Magnus at the battle of Kalveskindet, near Nidaros, in 1179, where Erling, who for about 20 years has been Norway's ruler, is slain.

From now on Sverre defeats Magnus in every encounter; Magnus' men are given the name of "Heklunger." The last engagement between the two is the bloody naval battle at Fimreite in the Sognefjord, 1184, and though Magnus had the supremacy in both ships and men, the battle ended in the defeat and death of Magnus and with him many of Norway's best men. Sverre is now sole king of Norway. But this does not end the civil wars. One group after another rises against him, and finally Sverre comes into violent conflict with the clergy. Most dangerous of all his clerical enemies was the scheming Bishop Nikolas Arnesson, a son of Arne of Stoddreim and Queen Ingrid, widow of Harald Gille. Nevertheless Sverre compels Bishop Nikolas and the three other bishops to crown him in Bergen and to swear him allegiance (1194). But no sooner is this done, when Bishop Nikolas leaves for Denmark, organizing there a new party, known as Bagler (from bagall, a bishop's staff). At the head of this party he places Inge, a pretended son of Magnus Erlingsson. And now the struggle continues between the Bagler and Sverre until 1202. Sverre seizes the

Slotsberg at Tunsberg, the main stronghold of the Bagler, but dies the same year.

What had Sverre accomplished? He had over-
thrown the monarchy lawfully created by Erling
Skakke in 1163, which really only established the domination of the barons and clergy, and he had restored
the monarchy as founded by the law of St. Olav: that
the king derived his authority from God; that he was
king of the whole nation, and upon him rested the duty
of maintaining law and justice for both great and small;
and that every male descendant of Harald Haarfagre
had the right to his share of the kingdom, whether born
in or out of wedlock. This last principle bearing on
the right of succession, was yet to do much mischief,
as will be seen.

Sverre had three children, Sigurd Lavard, already
dead, Haakon, and a daughter, Kristina. Besides, he
had a sister, Cecilia, married to Baard of Rein, a man of
power in the Trondhjem district. Haakon Sverresson
now mounts the throne and reigns from 1202 to 1204,
but dies suddenly, supposedly childless. He is succeeded by Gutorm, son of Sigurd Lavard. But now the
Bagler rise up again, spurred on by Bishop Nikolas.
This arch intriguer helps Erling Steinveg, another pretended son of Magnus Erlingsson, to bear the ordeal,
and proclaims him king of the Bagler faction. Gutorm
Sigurdsson dies the same year (1204) and as it is not
known that King Haakon has left any sons, Inge
Baardsson is chosen king, he being of the lineage of
Harald Haarfagre on his mother's side. But the Bagler will not be ruled by Inge, and the warfare continues.
There are many gruesome incidents. Worst was the
"bloody wedding" at Nidaros. In the winter time,
while Inge was celebrating his sister Sigrid's wedding,
the Bagler burst in on the festivity, ravaged and burnt,
killing many a doughty Birchleg. Only half dressed,
King Inge saved himself by swimming over the Nid
river, but was sickly from that time on. He now shared

the government with Haakon Galen (see genealogical
table, p. 87), later with Skule Baardsson, his half brother
on his father's side.   In the meantime the struggle
continues between the Bagler and the Bichlegs. Erling
Steinveg dies, 1207; thereupon Bishop Nikolas has his
nephew, Filippus, chosen king by the Bagler. Before
long, however, the two parties, wearied of the struggle,
form an agreement. Fillippus received Viken and Oplandene and married Sverre's daughter, Kristina. Filippus dies in 1217, and this event marks the end of the
Bagler faction.

But as early as 1204, shortly after Inge Baardsson's
accession, it was discovered that Haakon Sverresson
had a son. His mother was Inga of Varteig, whose son
was born shortly after Haakon's death, at the home of
the priest, Trond, at Eidsberg, Smaalenene. Fearing
the Bagler, she induced Trond to take herself and child,
— whom she named Haakon for his father — to King
Inge at Nidaros. After many dangers and hardships
they reached their destination and were well received
by King Inge. Haakon grew up under the care of King
Inge, and the Birchlegs were very fond of him. At
times they took hold of him and stretched him, saying,
"we will make you taller; you do not grow fast
enough."

7. *From the Death of Inge Baardsson (1217) to the Death
of Skule Baardsson (1240).*

King Inge died in 1217, Haakon Haakonsson being
then 13 years of age. According to St. Olav's law,
none had so good a right to the throne as he. But now
there is also another law, namely "Erling Skakke's
law," as we may call it for the sake of brevity (the law
of succession of 1163). This is in fact the law against
which Sverre and the Birchlegs have fought so hard;
but the survivors of the Heklunger and the Bagler fac-
tions, the clergy, especially the archbishop and the
flagellant monks at Nidaros, still held to this law. Ac-

cording to this law there are still several to be counted as "Pretenders." First of all Skule Baardsson, legitimate brother of King Inge. Then Sigurd Ribbung, who claimed to be the son of Erling Steinveg, pretended son of Magnus Erlingsson (see genealogical table, p. 87). Again there was Junker Knut, son of Haakon Galen (see table, p. 87). Finally, Gutorm, son of King Inge; but he was born out of wedlock, and his claim must preferably be referred to St. Olav's law, although he was not on the male side a descendant of Harald Haarfagre. The most formidable of these rivals was Skule Baardsson, because he was both powerful and able, and also very ambitious, besides, for several years he had been joint ruler with his half brother, Inge, who, in addition, shortly before his death had made Skule the commander of the royal bodyguard and given him the title of Jarl. Finally, shortly after Inge's death, Skule had assumed the government as Haakon's guardian. Skule hoped that he, as a man of experience, with the help of the clergy might be able to push the boy Haakon aside and himself be made king.

But the Birchlegs are on the alert. Through their efforts Haakon is proclaimed king at Øreting, and Skule for the time being has to make the best of it. Haakon gives him a third of the kingdom to govern independently, and he puts up with this arrangement for a while. At the death of Filippus, the last Bagler king, that same year (1217), Haakon is proclaimed king over all Norway, including Viken. But Skule is not satisfied, and the relations between him and Haakon are not good. A doubt is being raised as to whether Haakon is really the son of Haakon Sverresson, which before no one had doubted. And though Haakon could not but feel this as an insult, he agreed to have his mother prove her assertion by the ordeal. This she did in 1218. And this forms the opening scene of *The Pretenders*. On the same occasion it was also decided that Haakon should marry Skule's daughter, Margrete. Skule willingly consented to this arrangement, and the feeling between him and the king seems for a short time to be satisfactory. When a new faction, the Slitunger, stirs up a revolt in Viken the next year, it is quelled by Bagler and Birchlegs jointly. It now appears that the country will have peace. But the peace is of short duration. The following winter (1219-1220) there arrives from Denmark a young man named Sigurd. A flock gather round him, announce him as the son of Erling Steinveg, and accept him as king. This new party, also called the Ribbunger, and their king, Sigurd Ribbung, unite with the remnants of the Slitunger and harry the east country far and wide. It became Skule's task to subdue the Ribbunger; but its accomplishment was suspiciously slow. The old fox, Bishop Nikolas, gave reason to believe that he stood back of it all, and he certainly showed no willingness to help Skule against the Ribbunger. On the contrary he advised Sigurd Ribbung to come to an agreement with Skule. Sigurd renounced his title of king, Skule pledged him friendship and promised to plead his case before the king, with a view thus to obtain a part of the kingdom.

During the summer of 1222 the relations between Skule and the king again became strained. Skule collected taxes due the king, and when the latter advised him that this might become dangerous, Skule in anger went to Denmark early in the spring of 1223, seeking aid from Valdemar Seier against Haakon. On his arrival there he learned, however, that King Valdemar had been taken prisoner by one of his vassals, and thus he had to return with nothing accomplished. After Inga's ordeal (1218) no one had doubted Haakon's right to the throne. But another question arose: had he the sole right? Had not Skule and the other pretenders an equal right? This being whispered about, Skule was not slow to make use of any opportunity. Haakon was now 18, consequently of age, and had the right to rule without Skule's guardianship. On that

occasion a national assembly was held at Bergen in
August, 1223, attended by all of Norway's foremost
men.   But Haakon had decided that this assembly
should also act on his sole right to the throne, and with
that in view issued summons to all the other claimants.
Three of these pretenders appeared: Skule Baardsson,
Gutorm Ingesson, and Sigurd Ribbung, while Junker
Knut, the son of Haakon Galen, asserted his claim
through representatives.   But all voted for Haakon,
even the archbishop, who hitherto had shown coolness
towards Haakon.   The archbishop closed the meeting
by declaring that Haakon alone had the right by inheritance.   To Skule was now assigned the government of
the northern part of the kingdom, in extent not much
less than Haakon's share.   Haakon pledged to Gutorm
the affection of a kinsman.   Sigurd Ribbung and Junker Knut were not considered.

Skule went to Nidaros, taking Sigurd Ribbung with
him.   Though Skule had promised to watch him closely,
Sigurd soon found an opportunity to escape.   An Ice-
lander was found guilty of helping him and was executed.

Sigurd Ribbung again joins the Ribbunger, and Haakon had difficulty in weeding them out.   On the occasion when he seemed to have them in his power, he received a message from Skule that if he does not at once
celebrate his marriage with Margrete, Skule will consider their agreement broken.   Haakon therefore at
once proceeded to Bergen, where the wedding took
place, 1225.

That year Bishop Nikolas died.   On his deathbed he
called King Haakon and begged his forgiveness.   This
was granted and Haakon remained with him until he
died.

The relations between the king and Skule now
seem satisfactory; but soon there is another falling
out, and this time too it is caused by the Ribbunger.   It
appears that Skule supports the Ribbunger rather than

the king. Sigurd Ribbung dies in the spring of 1226; but now his faction chooses Junker Knut as their king, and not until 1227 does Haakon finally break their resistance. Junker Knut is pardoned and remains after that one of Haakon's most loyal friends.

For five years Skule keeps the peace; but he could not give up his ambitious dreams of once becoming king, much less when he learned that he had a son, of whose existence he had hitherto been ignorant. Skule's wife was Ragnhild, of the noted family of Giske, by whom he had several daughters. This son, Peter, was illegitimate, his mother being Ingeborg, the wife of Andres Skjaldarbrand. For the sake of this son, he now neglected both wife, daughters, and other kinsfolk; for his son was to ascend the throne after him.

His attitude toward King Haakon became more and more uncertain; twice, 1232 and 1233, Skule was summoned to a conference with the king, both meetings resulting in some sort of agreement, chiefly through Haakon's conciliatory spirit and leniency. — In the summer of 1236 the king and the Jarl again met in Bergen. On this occasion the jarl was given one third of Norway, and it was decided that they would live together for a period, in order thereby more easily to avoid gossip and misunderstanding. In the spring of 1237 they both went to Nidaros, and at Øreting Haakon conferred upon Skule the title of Duke, a title which no one had hitherto borne in Norway.

But Skule would not be satisfied with anything less than the royal title. In November, 1239, he broke all bridges behind him and had himself proclaimed king at Øreting. But there was little enthusiasm in the assembly, and the monks did not dare to bring out the shrine of St. Olav, which was the custom when a king was to be chosen. But Skule's son, Peter, took the shrine by force and bore it out to the assembly, against the protest and ban of the priests. Peter thus became guilty of church robbery, the most disastrous thing that he could have done to his and his father's cause.

When tidings of these happenings reached Haakon at Bergen he received them with his usual calm. "God be praised," said he, "now I know what henceforth I must do." Hardest of all was it for him to tell Margrete, who was both a loyal wife and a loving daughter. The first encounter between Skule's Varbelger and Haakon's Birchlegs occurred in March, 1240, near the river Laaka at Nannestad, not far from Oslo. The Birchlegs were led by Knut Jarl, who this time fell short of his old reputation as a warrior. His men took to flight as soon as the battle started, and Skule won an easy victory. But in April the same year Haakon himself at the head of his Birchlegs took Skule by surprise at Oslo, and after a fierce fight in the streets of the city, Skule was put to flight. He returned to Nidaros, but soon found that the sentiment had turned against him. This fact, together with his recent defeat, made Skule discouraged and uncertain. He lost all judgment and power to act, and when the fleet manned by Birchlegs, sent hurriedly from Bergen by Haakon, arrived at Nidaros on May 21, Skule was utterly unprepared and had to flee again. Abandoned by his men, he finally by the aid of some monks gained admission to the monastery of Elgeseter. Here he found his wife, Ragnhild. But the Birchlegs were in pursuit. In vain the archbishop pleaded with them to spare Skule; the Birchlegs would not listen; some of them even put fire to the monastery. Then King Skule came out; he held a shield before his face, saying only: "Strike me not in the face; it is not done with chieftains." These were his last words. Skule was slain at once. His son, Peter, had been killed a few days before. Here ends also the short saga of the Varbelger. And Skule's tragic death marks also the end of the 110 years civil wars.

When the message of Skule's death a few days later reached Bergen all were shocked, most of all Skule's daughter, Queen Margrete. Of all the characters in *The Pretenders* there is none that Ibsen has so masterfully described as Skule. He has perhaps exaggerated both his doubt and his sensitive respect for *right*, but otherwise he has undoubtedly given us a strikingly true characteristic of both the man and the deeds he tried to perform.

B. DRAMATIC POETRY

I.

How to Study a Drama.

1. A Drama Implies Action.

A drama differs essentially from both epic and lyric poetry. It is therefore self-evident that one cannot properly study a drama exactly as one does an epic or a lyric poem. Hence the study of a drama is not completed by a careful and precise mastery of the form and contents of every line. This necessarily belongs to the proper study of a drama, but just as much to the proper study of any epic or lyric poetry. Nor is the study of a drama completed by noting carefully how the different characters have been developed until one finally seems to understand them all. This too is absolutely necessary, but it is no less necessary in dealing with the general run of epic poems, novels, short stories, etc. This may all have been done without touching the peculiar and essential portion of a drama. What, then, is a drama? A drama is first and foremost action. That is why it is called drama, which means action. Hence, action is the real essence of the drama, that in which it differs from every other form of poetic art. A drama, we may say, is men in action, personages who act.

Thus, a drama is not properly studied and understood until it is studied and understood as action. For in the action lies the life or soul of the drama, and from the action springs what we call the main idea of the drama, the idea to which the author has sought to give a clear and graphic expression.

2. One Main Action.

But if the action of a drama is to give expression to one single fundamental idea, it follows of necessity that the drama must have only one action, that is to say, only one main action. Naturally a drama may have several actions; but they must all stand in a subordinate and subservient relation to the main action. There may also be many actors; but of them too it is required that they all — as personages in the drama concerned — stand in a subordinate and subservient relation to the person who carries or performs the main action. None of the various *dramatis personae* are present wholly on their own account, except the main personage.

3. One Leading Character.

From the unity of action follows again that the drama must have only one leading character. There may, as in *The Pretenders*, be two leading personages, but then each must represent one side of the main idea, and even then only one can be the leading character formally, that is to say, in reference to the form and structure of the drama. Again, this leading character may have many passions; but only one that dominates and rules, impelling him to action. Thus, out of a chaos of characters, actions and passions, a drama brings out a harmonious whole. A drama may be likened to a building, for example, a cathedral. In order to obtain a correct impression of a cathedral, we must not survey merely the parts one by one: the solid foundation, the white, gleaming marble, the splendid windows, the tall, conspicuous spire, etc. Each of these parts may in itself be very grand and beautiful; but it does not present to us the image of the great thought or idea, the revelation of beauty and harmony which the builder has sought to express. This only the cathedral as a whole can do. And so it is with the drama. We do not receive the correct impression of a drama nor see its greatness and beauty merely by studying the language, the style, the ideas of each speech, the characters; this we obtain only by viewing it as one great, harmoniously planned and executed action. A drama is so to say a living organism.

4. The Structure and Plan of a Drama.

A dramatist shows his art first and foremost in his method of construction, that is, in the plan and execution of his plot. And as all art — not least the dramatic — is an imitation and representation of nature and real life, his first and great commandment is: everything must be natural. Action in a drama must follow the same laws as action outside the drama, in real life. In all action of that sort we distinguish five different parts: cause, action in development, culmination, result, conclusion. Hence, ever since the time of Aristotle and down to Ibsen this quintuple division has been regarded as the perfect and only correct model in planning the action of a drama. Thus, the drama has been divided into the following five parts: exposition, rising action, climax, falling action, catastrophe. Shakespeare always followed this plan, and it is therefore usually called the Shakespearean plan: Ibsen followed it down to *A Doll's House;* from then on he went his own way. And as Ibsen now has won world fame just by the natural, realistic, and effective method of constructing his dramas, even those following *A Doll's House*, one may therefore no longer declare the Shakespearean plan to be the only correct and natural one. A great artist cannot be bound by certain, permanently fixed rules, however good and natural these may be.

But as Ibsen previous to *A Doll's House* has followed the Shakespearean plan throughout, hence, not only in

The Pretenders, but also in all his other works preferably read in our colleges. f. ex., *The Vikings at Helgeland, Brand, Peer Gynt, The League of Youth, Emperor and Galilean*, and *The Pillars of Society*, it might be worth while to consider for a moment this plan. The outline given below is based principally on *William Fleming, Shakespeare's Plots*, Chapter II.

II.

The Shakespearean Plan.

1. The Exposition or Introduction.

This must: a) Form the basis of the action to come, presenting to us the situation, so that when the action begins we may see that it has developed naturally from the assumptions and causes set forth in the Introduction. It gives us also the first immediate impression of several, perhaps the majority, of the personages appearing in the drama, first and foremost the leading characters.

b) It must, so to speak, win our interest, keep our mind tense in expectation of what is to happen.

c) Finally, it must be so constructed as to "foreshadow, perfectly and lucidly, the action of the drama."

2. The Rising Action.

The rising action begins where the introduction ends, and its function is to bring the action to a point where the principal character, as a result of the situation created by the preceding episodes, is impelled to make a decision, to commit an act which forms both the climax and the turning point of the entire action of the drama. This point, or act, is called the climax. Both in the *rising action* and the *falling action* there is a distinction between: 1. The main actions, usually performed by the principal character and leading directly by successive steps to the climax. 2. Sub-actions, which without directly serving as steps in the development, prepare and lead up to them. (For example, when Inga of Varteig brings Priest Trond's letter to the dying Bishop Nikolas). 3. Episodes that formally have no connection with the development of the action and thus might be omitted without spoiling the connection, but nevertheless are very useful, serving in the first place to check the action in order that the climax may not be reached too soon; in the second place to throw light on this or that personage or action, in short, to strengthen and enrich the movement. (For example, the women's conversation in *The Pretenders*, Act I.).

3. Climax.

Climax properly signifies a ladder, but denotes here the culmination or turning point in the action. It may consist of a single act (as in *The Pretenders:* Skule is acclaimed as Haakon's rival king) or of several acts combining as it were into one act (as in *Peer Gynt*, when Peer first abandons Solveig and soon after leaves his mother and the country).

4. The Falling Action.

The falling action moves from climax to catastrophe, showing us the natural and necessary consequence of what has happened in the rising action and the climax. Here too subsidiary actions and episodes are required.

5. Catastrophe.

Catastrophe means properly an overturning; then also a sudden and violent change, final event, outcome. Used in this sense it denotes the final solution of the plot, the conclusion of the entire main action with reference to the principal character. The catastrophe must be a natural consequence of what goes before. The catastrophe thus becomes dark or light, tragic or joyful, according to the situation the poet has brought about through the action. Sometimes, as in *En Fallit* and in *The Pillars of Society*, the catastrophe turns out to be light, though we feared it might be dark. It would have been a great mistake if the dramatist had not in the two plays mentioned allowed us to hope that it might be bright.

C. THE DRAMATIC STRUCTURE OF THE PRETENDERS.

In conformity with the plan outlined above, a drama should preferably have five acts, so that the exposition is the main feature in the first act, most of the rising action in the second act, etc. There are, however, several exceptions to this arrangement, even in Shakespeare. But *The Pretenders* answers this requirement as it does that of the above mentioned quintuple division.

I. The Introduction.

When the curtain rises in *The Pretenders* we learn at once that Inga of Varteig bears the glowing iron to prove that Haakon Sverresson is the father of her son, Haakon. And while waiting for the result, we make the acquaintance of Haakon Haakonsson and Skule Baardsson, the two most prominent of the four pretenders present, each claiming the right to the throne. And in true Shakespearean style the author in the very first speech they utter lets both of them express their fundamental characteristic: Haakon, assurance and faith, Skule, distrust and doubt. Inga having successfully endured the ordeal, Haakon considers this sufficient proof of his sole right to the throne, for he alone is born of royal parentage (see the *Historical Introduction*). But, when Haakon expresses his joy that he now has free hands, which he has looked forward to with such intense longing, Jarl Skule replies that he and the other two pretenders, Sigurd Ribbung and Gutorm Ingesson, have had the same reason for longing, for they too have sat with their hands tied. Haakon at first can hardly believe his own ears; but then Skule affirms frankly that the import of the ordeal was only to prove that Haakon had the right to assert his claim on a par with the other three (or four) pretenders. Otherwise he would not even have been considered. And Bishop Nikolas maintains that Skule is right. "In truth the Jarl has good reason for his opinion." Many of Haakon's men led by Dagfinn, become angry and are ready to spring to arms; but Haakon bids them be quiet. Although for six years he has borne the title of king, and the ordeal has declared him the only legitimate heir according to the law of St. Olav, he is willing to be on equal footing with the other pretenders, to sound the assembly call, and to let the matter be decided by election.

But as the assembly gathers on the spot where the election is to be held, Bishop Nikolas says to Dagfinn Bonde: "All goes well, good Dagfinn, all goes well; but keep the Jarl far from the king when he is chosen; — see you keep them far apart." The Bishop is therefore sure of Haakon's election, and so are we. But we are sure of more than that. We have already learnt enough about Skule to know that he, even now, will not yield, but will venture "new tricks." Thus we know also what the following act will be: a struggle for the throne of Norway between Haakon and Skule. And we have received a clear indication of one thing more: that Bishop Nikolas will be the drama's main intriguer.

II. The Rising Action.

Having now guessed with assurance what the king's whole action will center about, it is not difficult to conclude — what is soon to be confirmed — that the rising action must aim at making the tension between Haakon and Skule so strong that the result will be an open rupture. Every following act, serving directly to increase the tension between the two, will form a step in the rising action.

(1) Haakon's first act, fateful in this respect, is his

appointment of Vegard Væradal to be governor of Haalogaland.

(2) In the beginning of Act II, Skule does something which bears serious consequences in the same direction: Skule, who still has the king's seal, sends, without the king's knowledge, a letter to Jon, Jarl of the Orkneys, who has a quarrel with Haakon, and impresses it with the royal seal.

(3) Then Bishop Nikolas begins his contribution to the action. The Bishop knows that if Skule is to stand firm in his opposition to the king, he will have to be primed, stiffened, and above all, be made to doubt whether Haakon after all, is in his right. For, despite his ambition and all his other faults, Skule has an almost irrepressible respect for justice; he will not act contrary to what he believes is right. This conscientiousness, this sense of right, must be killed, thinks Bishop Nikolas, and with this in view he harangues Skule in a speech which may be called brilliant, and of which the substance is: "there is neither good nor evil, up nor down, high nor low. You must forget such words. Fulfill your cravings and use your strength: so much right has every man." Finally he bluntly invites Skule to follow the example of Lucifer. In order to raise a doubt in the mind of Skule as to Haakon's right, he tells about the letter of Trond the priest, which, if it can be secured, will make it clear that Haakon is not the child that Inga of Varteig bore, but that a substitution has been made.

(4) When Haakon takes Skule to task for the letter to Jarl Jon, Skule is unable to produce the letter and too proud to say why; he defies the king and says that he will not give it up. The bishop's speech has had its effect.

(5) The result of this refusal is that Skule, on the king's demand, must surrender the royal seal to Ivar Bodde, the king's chaplain.

(6) But Skule knowing well that none other than Ivar Bodde has given Haakon the information about the let-

ter to Jarl Jon, talks in bitter terms to Ivar, and several of Jarl Skule's men bid him "look to life and limb." Ivar Bodde then feels compelled to resign his position and depart. He is in fact exiled by Skule.

(7) Haakon takes this very much to heart and orders to send for Vegard Væradal, in order that he may have at his side a trustworthy man to replace the one he has lost. But just then a message is received that Vegard is slain by Skule's friend, Andres Skjaldarbrand. And when Haakon demands that Skule avenge the murder, the Jarl replies that he must refuse this too. When Haakon declares that he will exercise justice in the matter, Skule "with an expression of alarm" says that there will be bloodshed on both sides. Then the bishop announces that Andres Skjaldarbrand "has taken the cross." — All this has taken place at the wedding of Haakon and Margrete. Haakon now ends the feast and prepares immediately to depart for Viken.

(8) But at this moment enters Skule's sister, Sigrid, who, having received the power of "seeing what other eyes see not," after her wedding night of blood at Nidaros, speaks in prophetic terms about the day when Skule "takes the crown."

(9) This, coupled with all that has happened previously, moves Haakon profoundly; drawing his sword he speaks with great determination: all the Jarl's men must take the oath of allegiance to the king.

(10) Bishop Nikolas and Skule again engage in conversation, and the bishop leads Skule to promise that if he finds that Haakon is not the rightful king he must yield the place, though Skule be forced to take his life. "Ay — ay — 'tis in this mood I like the Jarl," says the bishop.

(11) More than the first half of the 3d act centers about the death of Bishop Nikolas and what was said and done previously. It is full of episodes and sub-actions, and we can hardly point to other actions having a direct influence upon the already strained relations

between Haakon and Skule, except that the bishop lets
Skule burn Priest Trond's letter. Thereby Skule's
doubt becomes immovable; he can not expect greater
assurance than he now has. Why not act at once, if at
all! "Tonight! — I will take the stride; I will leap the
abyss!"

(12) Their meeting ends with this threat by Haakon:
"From to-morrow you must give up your power and
dignities in my hands, — we two can not go forward
together."

(13) Thereupon Skule is brought face to face with his
daughter, Queen Margrete, and her little son, Haakon;
on this occasion a strong appeal is made to Skule's
heart as well as sense of duty; but he will not listen.
We now feel that we are approaching the climax.
There are many such decisive moments, *turning points*,
in Ibsen.

(14) Skule and Haakon meet once more. Skule
wants them to divide Norway into two equal parts,
each holding his share as a free kingdom. Or that each
rule over Norway for three years. But Haakon refuses
all of Skule's demands.

III. The Climax.

We have now reached the climax. Clearly Haakon
explains to Skule that he (Haakon) is the only man
who can achieve the deeds now required of Norway's
king: to unite Norway into one people. This is the
"king's-thought" that has come to him from God,
which Skule can not realize. Skule listens "in uneasy
agitation," but declares that this thought comes from
the devil. And now it appears that the bishop's pro-
voking words have borne fruit. Skule is no longer honest. Under the pretense of opposing Haakon's "king's-
thought," thus defending the old system, he decides to
have himself proclaimed king ("Then must St. Olav's
circlet fall": he who bears it must die), and soon he
lets action follow words. Thus is the break between

Haakon and Skule accomplished, and the climax of the rising action is attained.

IV. The Falling Action.

In order to point out the various steps in the falling action, we must naturally first of all make clear what is expected as the end, or the catastrophe. Considering only the climax, we may say that three contingencies are possible: (1) The downfall of Skule; (2) the downfall of Haakon; (3) the reconciliation of Haakon and Skule. But considering also the rising action we shall soon be convinced that only the first alternative is probable: Skule will fail. Every act or event tending to weaken Skule becomes a step in the falling action.

(1) Skule's victory at Laaka is the first of these steps. The victory has not increased Skule's courage and strength, but rather added to his dejection and doubt. After Haakon had expressed his great "king's-thought," there rose in Skule the spontaneous conviction that Haakon is the right one. Therefore he should have been victorious. That Skule after all was the victor causes him to doubt whether there is any "certain law on high, that all things must obey."

(2) The next step is the conversation with Jatgeir the Skald. In this conversation Skule attains the full assurance that he is the keel of the ship and Haakon the mast. But he must be the mast. That is to say: he sees no other way than to steal Haakon's king's-thought. And this he thinks would be possible if he only had some one by him who would believe in him unflinchingly. But we have no faith in this. We see and know that the talk with Jatgeir has brought him one step nearer to destruction, since never before has he so clearly recognized that he is fighting for an unjust cause, never has he so clearly shown that he will not yield to what he knows and feels is right.

(3) But he does find a man who has absolute faith in him, and he is none other than his son. He now has an

heir to the throne, provided he wins. Now he really
appears to believe himself saved. But we know better.
Now they are both to fight for Haakon's king's-thought
as their own; but we know Skule too well to believe
that he can win, even for a short time, a victory
founded on falsehood. And Paul Flida's appearance
convinces us that Skule's courage has vanished as
quickly as it came.

(4) Then comes Skule's meeting with Haakon at
Oslo. Here Skule acts like a madman, orders his men
to slay Haakon's child wherever there is opportunity,
even in the queen's arms, whereupon he is condemned
to death by Haakon. Now, if not before, we feel certain that Skule's doom is near. What a contrast between the raging berserk and the calm, dispassionate,
but firm and resolute Haakon.

(5) We meet Skule again at Nidaros, sick, discouraged, and in despair. And Peter by his church robbery
estranges from his father's cause all those who had any
respect for what then was considered sacred.

(6) Then comes the 6th and last step. Abandoned
by all, Skule is on the point of pledging his soul to the
devil in exchange for his help (See Skule's talk with the
monk, Act V.).

V.　Catastrophe.

However, a gleam of atonement is cast over the
catastrophe. The promise made to the woman he loved
saved him. And now, for the first time, perhaps, in
his whole life, can he really pray. And thus he is
saved, though death is certain. Now comes the catastrophe: Skule's death. But preceding the catastrophe
are Skule's repentance and penitence, and this makes
his death, which otherwise would have been a pitiable
defeat, in reality a triumphal exit from the world.

D.　LANGUAGE AND STYLE OF THE PRETENDERS.

Almost every page of *The Pretenders* recalls the language and style of the old sagas. As is well known,

the majority of our sagas have been handed down by oral tradition. In the sagas we therefore find not the literary but the spoken language. Thus also in *The Pretenders*. All the personages appearing in the play speak a plain, simple and natural language, each in his own manner, just as we would expect upon learning to know the speaker's character. It is true that we find speeches that are hard to understand; but the difficulty lies not in the language. In point of language everything may be plain and straightforward; but the speaker may purposely now and then have expressed himself enigmatically, as when Jatgeir the Skald speaks of him "who doubts his own doubt." But Jatgeir was a skald and the skalds frequently used ambiguous expressions. Again, the style of the sagas is remarkable for its peculiar conciseness. This is especially due to the fact that the men of the sagas speak their mind in the shortest form possible. And clear, forceful thoughts expressed in condensed form results in conciseness (Compare Bjørnson's style.). The personages in *The Pretenders* speak in that manner. The speeches are mostly brief, but even the longer ones, as for example, the monologues of Skule and the bishop, are brief in proportion to the wealth of thought contained in them. We point especially to two speeches, short in form, but powerful in contents, by Ingeborg Skjaldarbrand. Perhaps never has a shorter tragedy been written than this: "These eyes have been but a rain-clouded sky for twenty years," and, "To love, to sacrifice all, and be forgotten, that is my saga."

As to poetic flight, it may seem that many of those speaking in *The Pretenders*, — for example, Skule, the bishop, Ingeborg, not to mention Sigrid, — have reached higher than is usual with the protagonists of the sagas. But as a rule the words fall straightforward, clear and pointed, and the sentences are plain, short, and concise, just as in the sagas.

E. THE PRETENDERS AND IBSEN.

As previously stated, *The Pretenders* is first and foremost a psychological drama. The historical apparatus has been to the poet merely a container for his own ideas and experiences. And there are many of these Ibsenian ideas and experiences in *The Pretenders*. First to be noted are Ibsen's ideas and beliefs in a *call*. And this is in reality one of the fundamental thoughts in all of Ibsen's dramatic production. Every human being is born to a certain task or mission in life. To express this life mission he uses both in this and in his subsequent works the term *call*, and it is of the highest importance for each one to find and follow this call, or as Peer Gynt is made to say, to ascertain "what Master meant with him;" but, as the Button-Moulder says: "He must divine it;" for "in default of divining the cloven-hoofed gentleman finds his best hook."

Also in most of the works preceding *The Pretenders* reference has been made to this call. While this term has not been used, we may readily understand that according to Ibsen's idea, it was Catilina's call to save Rome, Fru Inger's to save Norway, Hjordis' to stand as the strong, radiant "shield-maiden" by the side of Sigurd Sea-King, and Falk's finally to become a great poet by the aid of Svanhild. And that none of them attained their aspirations was partly — and especially — due to certain flaws in their personality, partly to external circumstances, an unpropitious fate. This is what Ibsen calls the discrepancy between ability and aspiration, will and possibility. But in *The Pretenders* this aspiration, and this will, is plainly named *call;* here we meet for the first time a man who not only sees and believes unflinchingly in his call, but also succeeds in performing the task which this call imposes upon him. Haakon Haakonsson does not for a moment doubt that he has received a call from God to make Norway one people, and therefore neither does he doubt that he — and he

alone — is the man to perform this task. And therefore he performs it.

Likewise in the next work, *Brand*, the call has the
principal role, and here Ibsen shows us especially the
supreme right of the call. Everything must be sacrificed for its sake, if necessary; and Brand sacrifices all.

Ibsen, too, for many years had faith in his call, the
poet's call. And as poet he "would teach the Norwegian people to think great things." But during the
five or six years immediately preceding his writing of
The Pretenders, this faith had been put to a severe test.
His literary efforts found no response among his people.
He had sent forth one work after another, among them
a masterpiece in the *Vikings at Helgeland*, but few, if
any, cared about them. There was plenty of petty and
offensive criticism, but no appreciation. — Furthermore, his financial condition the last few years had been
as wretched as it could be without verging upon actual
starvation. The theater of which he had been the director since 1857, the *Norwegian Theater* in Oslo, was
closed on account of debts. It seemed that he could not
succeed in anything. — However, all this adversity did
not break Ibsen. On the contrary it became, as he says
at the millennial celebration, "the sound, though bitter
draught, from which I, as poet, on the brink of my
grave, derived strength to struggle on in the broken
rays of daylight." This shows how strong must have
been the faith in himself. But of the depth to which he
had sunk in his "horror of doubt," he gives us the most
unequivocal testimony in both verse and prose. In him
as in Skule, doubt was as it were the element in which
he lived at that time.

But all his doubt and despondency seemed to have
ended abruptly after his meeting with Bjørnson in the
fall of 1863 at a song festival in Bergen. Bjørnson was
at that time just the sort of personality which Ibsen soon
after described and named Haakon Haakonsson: always self-reliant, sure of his case, dauntlessly striding

forward — to victory. And he understood, as we know, the art of inspiring others with courage. It is said that Ibsen coming home from this meeting wrote *The Pretenders* in the course of a few weeks (some say six, others, eight), and here we again meet both of them, Bjørnson as Haakon Haakonsson, and Ibsen as Skule Baardsson. But note that it is Ibsen as he was before meeting Bjørnson, not as he was when he portrays Skule. The observant reader will soon perceive that it would have been impossible for Ibsen to portray Skule, unless he himself had had similar experiences; but he will note also that he could hardly have portrayed Haakon, unless he himself had felt some of the same buoyant faith in his calling as Haakon did. Of course he could not be the poet of optimism and faith; that was Bjørnson's sphere. But as Jatgeir Skald says, there are many kinds of gifts that may cause men to become poets. And one of them is the "gift of doubt." After all, Ibsen had always thought of himself as the poet of doubt. But it is not only Haakon, Skule, and Jatgeir, that Ibsen needs in order to express what at this time lay heavy on his mind. There is one more who in this respect plays an important part, namely Bishop Nikolas. The bishop is not only the unscrupulous intriguer, the evil spirit, who throughout the entire rising action urges Skule on toward the final break. But through him, especially in the ghost scene, Ibsen has found occasion to deliver to the Norwegian people a philippic, the like of which they certainly had never heard before; they were soon to hear more of the same kind in the two succeeding works, *Brand* and *Peer Gynt*. Especially the well known passage, "while to their life-work Norsemen set out," etc., is as if spoken directly from Ibsen's heart, even though he may not himself have fully believed that the faults of which he accuses the Norwegians ("will-lessly wavering, daunted with doubt, etc.") necessarily are to be explained in this mystic manner: namely that it is the "Bagler-Bishop tending to his calling."

How much it concerned Ibsen to get the opportunity of saying this to his countrymen, we can see merely from the circumstance that the entire ghost-scene is rather a break than a necessary link in the natural development of the main action. But formally, or pursuant to the whole plan of the drama, this whole invective becomes a mere injection into the play. The ghost-scene becomes as it were a sideshow that the poet has arranged in order to exhibit something he has found important enough to assign a place by itself.

The Main Idea.

The main idea in *The Pretenders* must evidently be sought in connection with the main characters: Skule and Haakon. Formally, of course, Skule is the principal character; but in reality they both are principal characters: each of them represents his side of the main idea: Haakon, the positive, Skule, the negative. This main idea may be expressed in various ways. Focusing our attention only on Haakon and Skule, we can perhaps not express it in better fashion than Henrik Jæger: "The new era's king's-thought is victorious," and "there is no hope for him who can only re-enact the old saga." But all can not have the "new era's king's-thought," as Haakon had. Nor does it fall to the lot of everybody to "stand next to the king," as Skule did. The main idea must therefore be cast in a commoner mould, adapting itself to all types, not merely to those of the first magnitude like Haakon and Skule. And this form is easily found. Haakon had not only the great king's-thought, the great call; but also a firm faith in his call, hence he had the courage and strength, enabling him to solve the problem imposed on him by the call. And Skule's drawback was not so much the fact that he "could but work out the old saga afresh," but rather that he erred in his call, hence always remained the doubting, disheartened, and irresolute man, who wasted his life. Therefore the main idea may be expressed thus:

"He who finds his call and believes in it is strong and will accomplish his mission in life, but he who does not find his true call is weak, because he will always be tortured by doubt, and he will not be able to accomplish his mission in life."

The Pretenders may thus be said to be a splendid illustration of the well known passage in Welhaven's poem *Orpheus:*

> Saa jammer bringende er tvilens gru!
> Ved den alene kan vi alt forlise;
> selv tankens liv gaar tapt, som Eurydice,
> naar denne dæmon raader i vor hu.
> En gud i os har al vor stordaad øvet,
> en gud maa bringe os vor bedste skat;
> men tvil er avmagt og en søn av støvet,
> den fører nedad i den gamle nat.

> "Unmerciful is the horror of doubt!
> By it alone may we forfeit all;
> Even the life of thought perishes, like Eurydice,
> When that demon rules our mind.
> A god in us has wrought our best achievement,
> He alone to us must bring our richest treasure;
> But doubt is faintness, born of dust,
> Leading down to everlasting darkness."

GENEALOGY

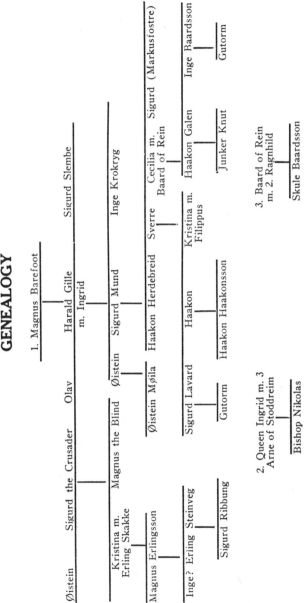

BRAND
Translated by Marie Malmin Meyer

BRAND

I.

"*Christ or Ibsen?*" is the title of a book published
in Norway about thirty years ago, written by a Norwegian pastor and fairly well-known critic. — "*Christ or
Ibsen?*" Of all severe judgments pronounced upon
Ibsen, surely the implication of this title is the severest.
From a Christian point of view, nothing can be more
completely annihilating. For this is, indeed, an uncon-
ditional either-or; the two are mutually exclusive.

And upon what is this severe judgment based?
Well, that is the strange thing. Not on works like *A
Doll's House, An Enemy of the People,* or *The Wild Duck,*
but upon *Emperor and Galilean* and — not at least to an
inconsiderable extent — upon *Brand.*

Upon *Emperor and Galilean* — well that doesn't
surprise us especially. For there at any rate *seems* to
be a great deal of ambiguous talk in that play. But
then, much depends upon how one, after the most unbiased study, understands these ambiguities and interprets the mysticism with which this work is so cram-
med, — interprets such mystic shibboleths as "the
third empire," "the tree of knowledge," "the wrath
of necessity," and so forth.

But more than all, it depends on how one understands Ibsen's personal relationship to the words
spoken by the *dramatis personae,* especially the Mystic
Maximos and Julian himself. In other words:
whether one thinks he has a right to look upon these
men simply as the spokesmen for Ibsen's ideas. For if
that is the case, there cannot be the slightest doubt
that the above title is justifiable; then *Emperor and
Galilean* must surely be one of the most anti-Christian
works ever written. — But must one necessarily accept
this interpretation?

Can anyone with justice — without the most conclusive evidence — attribute to an author what this or that one of his *dramatis personae* says and does? To what remarkable consequences would not such an assumption lead us! Furthermore, Ibsen is reputed to have treated his characters quite objectively, and he repeatedly insisted that they should thus be understood. And in regard to *Emperor and Galilean*, a Danish author, H. Thaarup (for example), has a few years later reached exactly the opposite of the accepted conclusion. There is no *either-or* in this case, he says, but a resolute *both-and*. We are to listen to both speakers; for there is no contradiction.

But, as before said, we are not nearly so surprised to hear such a severe judgment pronounced on the basis of evidence in *Emperor and Galilean* as when it is also supposed to concern *Brand*. Then we hesitate. Such a conclusion must sound strange to any reader who has tried his best to study this work, and who believes that he has discovered what Ibsen really meant by it, and who — most especially — has not omitted the last pages in the book, but has read them, studied them, and regarded them as seriously as the preceding parts. For if one does not omit the last part, or try by every manner of means to explain it away, he will soon see that it cannot possibly have been Ibsen's purpose by this play to show men the way of salvation, to point out Brand as the ideal Christian — not to say the ideal pastor. If that had been his intention, there might be good reason to ask, "Christ or Ibsen?" And then we might also with safety say that *Brand* is the most unsuccessful poetic creation in all of Norwegian literature, — yes, in all the literature of the world, for that matter. One is convinced long before one reaches the closing episode that Brand was never intended to represent the ideal pastor — or indeed one deserving in any sense the title of curator of souls. One needs only to look at the fruits of his "pastoral" activity.

Ibsen's situation is today the same as Shakespeare's has been and for the most part still is: "So many minds — so many opinions," which in this case means: So many critics, so many interpretations. And as far as Ibsen, at least, is concerned, this applies not only to the understanding and interpretation of his works, but equally to attempts to explain wherein his greatness consists and what attitude he assumes toward Christianity.

In the opinions of many, Ibsen is first and foremost a profound and original thinker, the bold and powerful teacher of new thoughts and ideas. He is, in other words, first and foremost a philosopher, prophet, preacher; and is therefore classified with Tolstoy, Darwin, — yes, even with Nietzsche. Others find it completely senseless to speak of Ibsenish thoughts and ideas. There are of course ideas in Ibsen's works; but they are not original. It is not Ibsen who first thought them. They were all well known when Ibsen adopted them. And it was far from Ibsen's intention to pose as a herald of new ideas. No, Ibsen's greatness consists in his ability to fill these well-known ideas with a new and exuberantly rich life and — above all — with a "colossal" dramatic suspense. (W. Archer). In other words: Ibsen was the great poet, the powerful dramatist. That and "naught besides." He can be classed only with Shakespeare.

And these "many minds" meet us not least when there is a question of Ibsen's attitude toward Christianity. Indeed, especially there. And here one can often scarcely avoid the conclusion of the famous English proverb, "The wish is the father of the thought." If the critic is himself a freethinker (atheist), Ibsen naturally also must be made a freethinker, not only in the last period of his literary activity, the period of naturalism, but also when he wrote *Brand* and *Peer Gynt*. Why, Georg Brandes lets even Søren Kierkegaard conclude his activity as an atheist. Well, I sup-

pose one couldn't let the most profound philosopher
of the North end in any other way. The wish is the
father of the thought.

If the critic is himself a Christian, he naturally wishes
also this man, with the great influence which he has
and the still greater which he will attain, to be the same,
and so there will naturally follow one of two consequences: Either one is resentful because he does not
find the Christian point of view as clearly defined in
Ibsen as he could wish, — even finds much which
seems somewhat questionable, which at times seems
even to point to the very opposite conclusion; and consequently he repudiates all of Ibsen's work as heretical
and asks with the author of the aforementioned book:
Christ or Ibsen?   (Thus A. Schack and others).   Or
he is able to place the most charitable construction on
everything, to interpret the questionable in the light
of what to him appears unquestionable, and with un-
deniable clarity to reveal what Ibsen *really* thought and
believed; and in that case, Ibsen will appear great to
him, not only as a dramatic artist but as a Christian
(See f. ex., H. Thaarup).

One might mention also a third group, composed of
those who do not believe that one can prove from
Ibsen's works any personal attitude toward religious
matters (either negative or positive); who think that
Ibsen is perfectly unbiased. "If anyone can extract
from all Ibsen's works his personal belief about God
or about man's relation to the unseen, all I can say is
that he can see further through a millstone than I can."
(W. Archer). In other words: atheist — Christian —
neutral — this is the sum and substance of all of it.
There are many things which might be said on this subject — indeed, it would be quite possible to write a
whole book about it; I can only remark that with re-

gard to Ibsen's *personal* Christianity, I am not in a position to express any judgment.

> It is not ours to search the heart and reins; —
> That is no task for dust, but for its ruler; —
>   (Funeral sermon in Peer Gynt)

But how anyone can read atheism into (or out of) works like *The Pretenders, Brand,* and *Peer Gynt* is to me completely incomprehensible. One might name many others as well, but especially these three.

That one person goes east and another west when it comes to understanding and interpreting these works in consequence of these circumstances goes without saying. But also in this connection one may distinguish definite tendencies among Ibsen readers.

We have, in the first place, those who may be called "racers," who do not study, but only read — and read fast — perhaps only one work here, one there, chosen at random. And they soon have their minds made up. Ibsen himself insisted — and it is the only suggestion that he gives about the reading of his works — that they should be read in chronological order. Only then will one be able to understand the individual work, and then only see the unbroken continuity of thought in all his works.

In the second place, we have the reader who looks through the spectacles of others, and there are more of them than one would expect. And in Norway and Denmark it seems to be the spectacles of Georg Brandes which have been put to the most frequent use. He has for so long a time been reputed the most ingenious critic of the North (cf. Thaarup's Henrik Ibsen, pp. 32 and 52). But in that case we can readily appreciate what will be the resultant understanding of Ibsen's works, and of his Christianity.

We may also distinguish between foreign (non-Norwegian) critics, Norwegian critics, and the common reading public.

As far as the foreign critic is concerned, he has this advantage over the Norwegian that it is easier for him to keep to the essential or universal in an Ibsen opus. As a rule, he has neither a detailed knowledge of or a special interest in what may be called its Norwegian appeal — that aspect of the work which principally concerns Norway and Norwegians, and Ibsen's personal relationship to the Norwegians at the time the work was composed. And in most of Ibsen's works there is just such a Norwegian aspect, of greater or lesser prominence. — Therefore it is often fully as profitable to read a foreign critic as a Norwegian on matters dealing with the kernel or central theme of a play.

For, as is reasonable, a Norwegian critic is in constant danger of losing himself completely in the Norwegian elements of the work, so that one is almost led to believe that he either cannot or does not wish to see anything but what especially concerns Norway and Norsemen. Thus in the case of *Brand* and *Peer Gynt*, it may happen that he gets no further than to prove how these works are a kind of "thanks-for-past-favors" from Ibsen to his countrymen, how Ibsen was feeling when he wrote them, and how they came to be written; how he in the pastor in *Brand* has wished to depict a man who is completely characterized by those traits which he especially missed in the Norwegians of the 60's, and in Peer Gynt a Norwegian as he actually was at that time — in Ibsen's opinion. Yes, at times it seems as though Henrik Jæger himself has been unable or unwilling to see more than that. And less than a year ago was published *Henrik Ibsen's Brand*. The book is written by Just Bing, and is consequently both interesting and instructive — in its own way. It throws light on many things which have to do with the origin of the work. And that, indeed, is the purpose of the work, and so it gives little or no help toward an interpretation of the essential and universal truths of Ibsen. Indeed, I am inclined to say, less than nothing, as far as the last act (and especially the last scene) is concerned.

Among the ordinary readers, "laymen," as we in this connection may call them, there are probably many, very many, who never read Ibsen, and among those who read him, again many who read him with little understanding — as is to be expected; the majority of Ibsen's works must be read not once, but repeatedly — they must be *studied;* but then among these "laymen" there are also some who with respect to the essential theme — the "message," — read with an understanding which might well be the envy of many a scholarly critic. But how is that possible? Well, in the first place, they are sufficiently "naive" to read and study the *work* itself as a piece of literature. They have often little or no opportunity to read *about* the work. And so they read the work *itself,* not allowing others to dictate to them how they should interpret it. In other words, they read with their own spectacles.

And I wonder if we do not right here find the two most important reasons for the fact that there has been and still is so little understanding of Ibsen and what he really intended: (1) we read too much *about* Ibsen and too little *of* Ibsen; (2) and we do not do our own reading, but let others read for us. Of course, that is true not only with respect to Ibsen, but more or less to all writers who are — or at least have a reputation for being hard to understand.

Of course, I do not mean to say that one should not read *about* Ibsen and his works or that one should altogether avoid notes and commentaries. Quite the contrary! Most of Ibsen's works — in fact, all the greater compositions of whatever author — are of such a nature that if one is to get a complete and comprehensive understanding of them, one needs help both from the literary critic and from history — first and foremost from literary history. And so the more real aids one can make use of, the better.

But one must not forget to read the works, and to read them *himself*. And to do that first and foremost. It seems that our day and age needs especially to be admonished on this point. For is it not a conspicuous fault of our age that men want to read, but especially (or only) such things as require no study, — that they want to get thoughts, but not think them themselves? Therefore there are so many who never get beyond newspapers and magazines. There the thoughts lie ready for the taking. And that sort of reading seems actually to obtrude itself upon one from all directions. And unfortunately, it seems also as if this weakness of keeping to newspapers and magazines — to light reading altogether — is not most prominent among young people.

And with respect to Ibsen and his works, there is a special reason for such an admonition about "reading first the works," and that reason is that there have been and are so many of these destructive critics who with beak and claws want to make Ibsen profitable for themselves, by giving their readers the idea that he and they are as one. By reading the actual works, and by reading them oneself, one might happen to arrive at exactly the opposite conclusion.

II.

It is in the spirit of these lay critics that we shall in what follows try to read and to interpret Henrik Ibsen's *Brand:* we shall try to let the drama speak for itself. And we shall also try to let the drama answer in its own words such questions as: Is Ibsen in this work just a' poet, or just a moralist, or both? Is it an atheistic or a Christian attitude toward life upon which it is founded? I believe it is the very popular literary critic Hippolyte Taine who has taught that by studying f. ex. a work by Shakespeare we learn to know not alone the great author, but also his generation, the age and environment in which he lived, and so forth. Now, we

are far from agreement with Taine in looking upon a
work of art as purely a product of the age in which it
was produced; but in the case of many works —
whether of Shakespeare or of some other great poet —
there is not a little truth in the statement.

1. The Norwegian Aspect of Brand.

In most of Ibsen's works there is a specific Norwegian element; that is to say, there is something especially addressed to Norway and Norwegians, which, in
other words, particularly concerns them. In some this
is less obvious, in others more. To the latter class belong *Brand* and *Peer Gynt*, not to mention the Norse historical plays, such as *The Pretenders*, *The Vikings*, and
Fru Inger.

Especially noteworthy is this particularly Norwegian
appeal in *Brand*. And consequently we shall in studying this play need all the help we can get from both the
political and the literary history of Norway.

When it is so frequently remarked that Ibsen was
very wroth with the Norsemen as he saw them in the
sixties, and that he then created the pastor Brand to
show them how they *ought* to be and Peer Gynt to
show them how they really were, there is in the statement a certain element of truth, but it is by no means
the whole truth. It is true that Ibsen was dissatisfied
with the Norsemen in the sixties — yes, in one sense,
he was dissatisfied with them as long as he lived for that
matter. It is also true that when Ibsen wrote *Brand*
and *Peer Gynt*, it was his primary intention to pass
judgment upon the Norsemen. But when many aver
that this was his whole and only intention — or practically so — one can scarcely do him a graver injustice.
For then he reduces these ingenious works of dramatic
art, the greatest in the whole literature of the North,
great even in the literature of the world, — then one
reduces them to a group of ill-tempered jobations, to
mere ephemera, that were possibly of some value to the

Norsemen of the sixties, and that still may be of interest to the social historian as monuments of cultural history, but which are of indifferent importance to the rest of the world. For of what possible interest could it be to an Englishman, a German, a Frenchman, an American, etc., to see what sort of creatures the Norsemen were some seventy — eighty years ago? But what do we see? Why, we discover that as time goes by, these works become but the more highly regarded — not alone in Norwegian literature, not alone in Northern literature, but also — we may safely say — in world literature.

Ibsen has, then, in both these plays known how to accomplish two things at once. He has, in the first place, sent a special greeting to contemporary Norsemen, has succeeded in laying before them the matters with regard to them which especially concerned him — and that is not such a trifle. And, in the second place, he has spoken to all human beings, regardless of where they dwell and to what nation they belong, words which are significant for all times, — truths of universal and eternal validity. And herein lies the greatness, the ingenuity of these works as in all first class works of art. That he has disciplined his compatriots, punished them until they smarted, that is not a trifling accomplishment; but others could have done so — have indeed done so, although not so severely. But that he at the same time could speak in such a way that his words have validity for all that is called humanity, so that everyone, whatever his native home, might see himself mirrored in his words, that is a thing which only a poet of true genius could do. Ibsen's works have therefore with striking appropriateness been compared to the fishing tract of the *hulder* with its double bottom. Above one partition, one thing is said; but below, one hears — not necessarily something essentially different — but an echo of something more, something of far greater significance. A foreigner may thus read *Brand* and *Peer*

Gynt with practically the same profit as a Norseman, even if he doesn't know a particle about contemporaneous Norsemen and Ibsen's opinion of them — if only he understands human nature. And such an understanding is a prerequisite for every Ibsen student.

But first — or to continue the figure, above the upper partition, just below the surface of the water — Ibsen addressed himself especially to the Norsemen of the sixties, and, as before remarked, he has a great deal to say to them. And to all who undertake to *study Brand*, and who want to learn *all* that Ibsen intended that his work should teach, it must be of considerable interest to be able to distinguish between what is especially applicable to Norsemen and what is of universal applicability. And to us who are of Norwegian descent, this must be of especial interest, because it may well be that one thing or another that Ibsen mentions here may throw light upon certain passages in our history and certain aspects of our personality. It must, of course, be admitted that Ibsen's accusations against the Norsemen of the sixties and especially their leaders and officials are often exaggerated, so that now and then they are little short of caricatures; but some truth there must surely be in these accusations and some resemblance in these caricatures. And if that is the case, they can no longer be a matter of indifference to us.

We shall first, then, look at *Brand* in its national frame, or in other words: we shall look at the *pastor* Brand as the disciplinarian of the Norsemen.

Ibsen was incensed at Norway and the Norwegians when he started off on his first journey abroad in 1864. And his wrath was the more burning and his indignation more deep for the very reason that he loved his country and his countrymen above all others. For that Ibsen, in spite of everything, loved Norway and the Norwegians is now apparent from many things, perhaps preeminently from some of his poems, as f. ex., *Burnt Ships*, which closes with these lines:

From the sun-warmed lowland,
Each night that betides,
To the huts of the snow-land
A horseman rides.

But Ibsen found himself in the same dilemma as Brand:
he had to strike when he wanted to caress; he had to
reprimand when he longed to praise and admire.

And when he now through a long period of years in
one play after another: *Brand, Peer Gynt, The League
of Youth, Pillars of Society,* and so forth, is engaged in
reprimanding the Norwegians, his motive is in all prob-
ability the same as that of Brand: he lifts high the
banner of idealism in order to make a true "aristocracy"
of his countrymen — an expression he uses himself in
Rosmersholm. That was what he, according to his own
statement, looked upon as his whole business of life:
to get his compatriots to "think nobly." That this feeling was at first not unmixed with personal bitterness
cannot be denied and cannot indeed be wondered at; but
surely no one can seriously believe that a personal feeling was the motivating influence in his long disciplinary
activity. One does not work a whole generation to raise
and ennoble a people merely as a revenge for a personal
grudge.

It was early in the spring of 1864. Since the fall of
1857, Ibsen had been resident in Christiania.* And
these six-seven years had been the hardest in his life, —
in many respects. His economic condition had been as
bad as it well might be without his actually starving to
death. Matters finally came to such a pass that every
stick of furniture in the house he rented had been
pawned, and some of the few friends he had seriously
tried to get him an appointment in customs in order that
he might have daily bread.

For it had not fared well with his work in Christiania.
He had begun in 1857 as director of "The Norwegian
Theatre," and it can hardly have been the fault of the

*Oslo.

director only that this theatre had to close its doors in
1862. Then he secured a position in the "Christiania
Theatre"; but the salary (three hundred dollars a year)
was not enough for a family father either to live or to
die on. In 1860, he had together with Bjørnson and
Vinje applied for a traveling stipend. Bjørnson and
Vinje were granted theirs; Ibsen was not. Well, that is
to say, in 1862, he was granted a small sum of money
(100 kroner, a little more than $25), to enable him to
go to Western Norway to collect folk literature, and it
is said that it was on this journey that he saw the place
which became the prototype for the parsonage in
Brand.

But in his literary activities so far, Ibsen had been least
successful. He had written some things, such as *The
Vikings at Helgeland;* they had brought him little or
no recognition, but a great deal of adverse criticism.
He had written *The Comedy of Love;* but a professor
at the University had declared that a man who could
write a thing like that ought to have a sound thrashing
rather than a stipend. In his later writing he had given
voice to a new and, as he thought, truer interpretation
of life than the romantic. No one would listen. He
had pointed to faults and shortcomings in the individual
as well as in society. He was not understood.

But then — at the close of the year 1863 and the beginning of 1864 — came the climax of this tragedy.
For it was then that Germany deprived Denmark not
only of Holstein, but also of Slesvig, which from time
out of mind had belonged to Denmark. And neither
Norway nor Sweden came to the help of their brother
— in spite of many high-sounding speeches which the
academic youth from both of these countries had in-
dulged in, and in spite of many toasts which the same
academic youth had drunk to the unity of the three
Northern nations in time of trouble. But they stayed
quietly at home. That Norway and Sweden did not
meddle in the one-sided struggle was undoubtedly good

diplomacy. And, of course, neither the Norwegian nor the Swedish nations, nor their official representatives had made any promises. But what did the idealist Ibsen care about diplomacy and official formalities when it was a case of moral duty and national honor? Even if Norway had as a result of interference lost her national freedom and independence, what did that matter? he thought; they could surely regain that. But for this breach of moral responsibility they could never atone, and this blot upon the national honor they could never erase. That the Norsemen on this occasion remained quietly at home was for Ibsen the bitterest disappointment of his life. He never forgot it. And assuredly he did not forget it when he was writing *Brand*.

In the spring of 1864, Ibsen had finally succeeded with much difficulty in getting a stipend which enabled him to reside for one year in a foreign city. And Ibsen started off. He wanted to go to Rome, and his way took him through Germany. In Berlin he witnessed an event the very thought of which he says came near to driving him insane. He saw the triumphal return of the Germans after their victory over Denmark, saw the Germans spit upon the war-trophies which were stained with the blood of his suffering brethren — the brethren whom his compatriots had refused to aid.

Then Ibsen came to Rome, and there we find him a year later, in the summer of 1865. What had he been doing in the course of that year? He had worked and slaved over a subject which not only lay far removed from his own country and his countrymen, but also far removed from his own time — fifteen centuries removed, in fact. He had wanted to depict the last struggles of the doomed Graeco-Roman paganism and the triumph of the new and vigorous Christianity. He had, in other words, begun the work which he succeeded in completing some nine years later, — *Emperor and Galilean*. But at this time he had been unable to do any-

thing with it. He couldn't get his mind from his country and his people. He had to settle scores with them,
had to tell them what he thought of their attitude.

Then one day in the summer of 1865, during a visit
to the Cathedral of St. Peter, he got his idea for Brand,
the *pastor* Brand. Now he was in a position to read his
people a lesson, and to do it with both power and em-
phasis. Now he could depict a man who should be
strong in just that respect or those respects in which he
found the Norsemen weak, in which lay their fundamental flaws, and then he was going to let the Norsemen
stand as a contrasting background for this man. And
so he created the pastor Brand. So (he seems to say)
a *man* should look. Now compare yourselves with him!

This pastor Brand is far from being perfect. He is
not the kind of man who is always sure ahead of time
of what he ought to do or not do; he often errs in his
judgment. But when he sees that he has made a mistake, he is always ready to admit it; and when he thinks
that he sees the way he should travel, he goes that way,
even though he must go without kin and without
friends, hunted like a wild beast by those for whom he
has sacrificed everything that a human being holds dear
on earth. Never does he evade any demand which
comes in the name of duty or responsibility or sacrifice.

But in contrast to such a man, with his keen sense of
moral responsibility and his unbendable iron will, any
man (and not only any Norwegian) will look small and
insignificant, yes, like a pigmy or dwarf. In *Brand*,
Ibsen has indeed read his people a lesson. Never had
they suffered so severe a reprimand, unless it be in *Peer
Gynt*. It fairly rains accusations, jeers, and mockery
upon them from beginning to end.

But exactly what is the roll call of their sins according to Ibsen? It is a long catalogue with many entries.

But all these weaknesses have one root, one common
source. All of them come from the disastrous desire to
excuse themselves, to evade all demands which entail

any kind of sacrifice, whether in the form of money or (and especially) of some noble and unselfish deed, some deed which is done preeminently for the good of *others*. We are so few in number and so insignificant, they say; we live in a barren land far to the North. We have enough, yes, more than enough, to do to take care of ourselves. Therefore no one has a right to demand anything of us. The bigger and richer nations farther south — of them you can make your demands. They can give, but not we. Thus the mayor says to Brand:

> Here you'll scheme in vain!
> Out in the great world that may stand; —
> Go thither with your big demand,
> And let us plough our moors and main.
> [Herford trans. Act. III, p. 104]

And then you must not forget, the Norsemen say to all who make demands, that we have some quite distinguished ancestors. They could sacrifice, and they have sacrificed — both for themselves and for us.

> MAYOR.
> We also flung our mite into
> The world's great treasure of bold deed.
> True, that's long since; but, after all,
> The mite was not so very small.
> Now the land's dwindled and decay'd
> But our renown still lives in story.
> The days of our reported glory
> Were when the great king Bele sway'd.
> . . . .
> Nay, legend names a lion-hearted
> Hero that took the cross; in verity,
> It is not mention'd that he started —
>
> BRAND.
> He left behind a large posterity,
> This promise-maker?
> MAYOR.
> Yes, indeed;
> But how came you to — ?
> BRAND.
> O, I read
> His features clearly in the breed
> Of promise-heroes of today,
> Who take the Cross in just his way.
> [Act III, pp. 102-3]

But in the midst of his wrath and indignation, Ibsen
has tried to be just. He has not laid the principal blame
for all this unwillingness to give and this passivity upon
the common people. No, the chief accusation and the
real sting of all the jeers and irony of the play are directed against the official class, against those who should
be the leaders of the people, and by precept and example guide them forward and upward, but who actually
are doing the very opposite:

> They have drained its (the Norwegian people's) best blood,
> Have taken the marrow from their courage;
> They have broken into bits
> Every soul that should have stood like steel.

But about the Norwegian officials; — haven't they
for a long time had a reputation for honesty and up-
rightness? Yes, indeed. And even Brand gives them
in his own way a testimonial to that effect. He says
about the Mayor:

> A people's champion, thorough-bred!
> Active, with fair and open hand,
> Honest of heart and sound of head,
> But yet a scourge upon the land!
> . . . .
> How many a thought is cleft,
> How many an eager will made numb,
> How many a valiant song struck dumb
> By such a narrow soul as this!

How then, we may ask, is this apparent contradiction
to be explained? By the fact that the officials do not
stand in the right relationship to the common people. In
their own way, they desire the good of the people. In
their own way — like the Mayor, they can even lead
them in matters pertaining to material progress. But
they are first and foremost concerned with the performance of every jot and tittle of the duty which according to statute belongs to their office. And when they
have done that, then they have also satisfied the full demands of life. Then neither God nor man can ask more
of them (here one might cite numerous instances). So-

cially they consider themselves far above the "common horde." They are the fine folk, those who are possessed of all that can be called culture, and it never for a moment occurs to them to try to come in closer contact with the common people, to share the cultural and educational advantages with them, to elevate and ennoble, to direct them toward higher ideals, and so forth. The "plebeian" *is supposed to be* as he is, stupid and drab, — lacking in individuality. For then he is most easily manageable for the officials, and then they can better feel their superiority to him (see, f. ex., the Dean's replies to Brand, some of which are quoted below).

Well, we know that at least when this play was written, there was not a little truth in these accusations. But we know also that this social cleavage was an inheritance from the time when most of the officials — and especially those of higher rank — were Danes, spoke Danish, lived upon Danish culture, had their cultural center in Copenhagen, and felt themselves far superior to the Norwegian peasant and the Norwegian fisherman, who spoke Norwegian and held fast to Norwegian cultural ideals, a heritage from the "days of glory now long past," but a heritage far greater than any of those who had existed chiefly on foreign influences could conceive of, a heritage brought to light and to appreciation by romanticism: folk literature, folk music, folk art, folk lore and customs, folk history, etc., which gave the final blow to the great "progress" to which the second half of the 18th century had been witness.

And we know also that this heritage will come into its own, that little by little it will fill this cleft between official and plebeian as well as other clefts in the Norwegian social strata. And so now one may say openly that there is not nearly so much truth in these accusations as there was some 60 or 70 years ago.

But Ibsen lays the blame especially for this unfortunate state of affairs upon the institution called the established church, that (in his opinion) perverted image of a *true* church, that institution which instead of making its members thinking, self-determinant, responsible person-ages actually seems to make a special effort to reduce them to a homogeneous gray mass of which it may be said that:

> His individuality must each man tame,
> Not elevate himself, nor stand out,
> But obliterate himself in the crowd.
>
> . . . .
> For every man the same step forward,
> For every man the same pace, —
> See, that is the ideal in this plan.

The Dean, who represents the established church, has a keen eye for his own good, as well as for that of the State, but is stone-blind when it is a question of spiritual guidance. When Brand, who has just built a new church, maintains that:

> A House new-builded asks, as well,
> A cleansed Soul, therein to dwell.

the Dean replies:

> All that will come without our stir.
> So gay, so elegant a roof
> Will be an adequate reproof
> To every unwash'd worshipper.
> And that delightful sounding-board,
> That doubles every pious word,
> Will render without fail our flocks
> Fivescore per cent more orthodox.

These are, in all brevity, the aspects of the national role wherein he has only Norwegians as a background. But if that were his only role, the whole work *Brand* would long ago have sunk into oblivion, would now, as remarked before, be of merely historic interest.

But the pastor Brand has also another part to play,

2. *The Universal Elements in Brand.*

and in that he has not only the Norsemen as a contrasting background, but all of humanity — all that can be called human beings. And in that part it is his task to

show humanity that there is something which may be
called the "ideal demand," and that this demand is sovereign, has absolute authority and validity. It is the *duty*
of all men to meet this demand, whether they can or not.
They need only listen to their own consciences to realize
that. They must at least be desirous of meeting it to
their utmost ability. If then they are unsuccessful, why,
"*that* can be forgiven, but never that you would not try."
It is our duty also to be able to comply; but to be able to
satisfy completely the demand is impossible; therefore
God will "forgive" us our lack of ability if we but *will*
what is impossible.

> First the Will
> Law's thirst for righteousness must still.
> You must first will! Not only things
> Attainable, in more or less;
>
> .   .   .   .
> No, you must will with flashing eyes
> Your way through all earth's agonies.

This is Brand's attitude at all times, from the time we
first meet him until he is through with the "Cross" and
"The Phantom," — that is to say, throughout the work
with the exception of the last 120 lines. Brand becomes
then what we might call the champion of the ideal demand. But not only that. He is not only the champion
of the ideal, but also one who himself struggles to attain it as far as he is able, but whether his grasp equals
his reach, — well, we shall see that later. But it is his
struggle toward the ideal that makes him so interesting
and the play so instructive.

This is, then, Brand's primary objective: he is the
champion of the ideal. And this objective has at all
times the same validity. It can never become out of
date as long as human nature is what it is.

But although this whole work (excepting always the
last 120 lines) concerns itself entirely with an ethical
or moral problem, not a religious, it is nevertheless significant that Brand is a pastor, because this precludes

any uncertainty on our part as to the meaning of the "ideal" or the "ideal demand." These words upon his lips can mean nothing less than *God's Will* as it is revealed in his holy commandments.

At the beginning Brand is far from being an ideal person. His self-righteousness and haughtiness are boundless. He does not know if he is a Christian, but he knows that he is such a man as a man ought to be. And he thinks that he has been placed in the world as a "physician for all sins and weaknesses of the world."

And as is the state of his soul or emotional life, so also is his understanding. He is always *groping* his way forward. Every now and then, he is forced to admit that he has erred. There is only one phase of his soul-life which is nearly perfect. That is his *will*. He *wills* to do the right whatever the cost. Therefore he is also honest — yes, fundamentally honest.

We can easily understand that just so Brand had to be in order to play the part that Ibsen had laid out for him. Had he not been so honest and so strong-willed, there would have been no conflict; he would at once have given up, as most persons do when the struggle becomes too severe. And if he had seen everything clearly beforehand, so that he had not had to grope, and if he had had a good and humble heart, he would have had nothing to struggle against, and nothing to strive to attain. He would have been too close to the ideal at the very beginning. But as it is, Brand's struggle to reach the ideal is the very core of the play, which keeps us in suspense, and finally makes us understand and like him. Had he not been so human, had so many frailties, his fate would have been that of many a hero and heroine of the novels and dramas of the past; they are angels, and we cannot discover that we have anything in common with them, and so we lose interest in them. His moral victories would not under such circumstances be of any significance to us ordinary folk.

Well, then, Brand is a young pastor, and a pastor he

wants to be for the whole world. For he is the "physician of the world." And his life's work is to make real
human beings out of all this rubbish which calls itself
humanity:

> From these scraps and from these shreds,
> These headless hands, and handless heads,
> These torso-stumps of soul and thought,
> A Man complete and whole shall grow,
> And God His glorious child shall know,
> His heir, the Adam that he wrought.
>
> [Act I.]

And his performance shall be so grand, his conduct
so glorious, his speech so overpowering that his generation of man would *have* to be transformed by it, to become a new race.

But before he sets out on this great mission, he wants
to visit his old home once more, a deep, narrow, sunless
valley in Western Norway. As he approaches his native village, he meets some persons who have come up
from the valley. First he meets the peasant and his son.
This peasant is on his way to visit a daughter who is
dying, but cannot die in peace before she has spoken
with her father. And he is willing to give all that he
owns to insure her a peaceful death. There is only one
thing which he will not give, and that is his own life.

Then he meets a newly engaged couple, Einar and
Agnes. With them, all is song and laughter; they are
completely content with everything; and they feel that
God has been good to them. Einar thinks God has been
"incomparably" good to him. He has in the first place
made him an artist, and then he has given him Agnes
for his bride. Now they are going to live their whole
lives in beauty, play, and joy, and then they expect to
go "home once more — to heaven."

Then he meets Gerd, a halfwitted gipsy girl. She is
perpetually rushing about in search of a big, ugly hawk,
which she thinks is always after her to hurt her. She

has completely broken with everyone and everything down there in the valley: with the people, with their customs and manners, with their form of worship, yes, even with their God. Up on the wild moors she has her own house of worship, the "ice-church."

> Yonder the cataract's singing Mass;
> There on the crags the whistling weather
> Preaches you hot and cold together.
> Thither the hawk will ne'er steal in.

Gerd knows no other law than her own desires.

These persons whom Brand has met symbolize for him three types of human beings. The peasant and his son represent "Faint-heart," Einar and Agnes, "Light-heart," and Gerd, "Wild-heart." And every one of those for whom he is going to be the "physician," belongs to one or another of these classes. He sees at once what these people are upon whom he is going to work the glorious transformation.

Most people would judge the peasant and his son, and Einar and Agnes to be respectable folk, whom Brand could easily transform. But Gerd, poor child, the wild and wayward gipsy girl, — it must be almost impossible to do anything for her. Brand's judgment is quite the opposite:

> Of dulness dulness is the brood, —
> But evil's lightly won to good.
>   [Act I.]

(Are we not involuntarily reminded of such words as: "Publicans and sinners will sooner enter into the kingdom of heaven than ye"?)

What Gerd undertakes, she does with her whole soul, never "in shreds and scraps." For it is just this half-heartedness, says Brand, which is the worst weakness of all. "All or nothing" is his slogan.

Well, Brand recognizes this "Call" clearly now: to fight against these three demons called "fainthearted-ness," "frivolity" and "wild-heartedness," the "fell triple-banded foe":

> Which wildest reel, which blindest grope,
> Which furthest roam from home and hope: —
> Light heart who, crown'd with leafage gay,
> Loves by the dizziest verge to play, —
> Faint-heart, who marches slack and slow,
> Because old Wont will have it so: —
> Wild-heart, who, borne on lawless wings,
> Sees fairness in the foulest things?
> War front and rear, war high and low,
> With this fell triple-banded foe!
> I see my Call! It gleams ahead
> Like sunshine through a loop-hole shed!
> I know my task — these demons slain,
> The sick Earth shall grow sound again; —
> Once let them to the grave be given,
> The fever-fumes of earth shall fly!
> Up, Soul, array thee! Sword from thigh!
> To battle for the heirs of Heaven!

The situation is then this: Brand believes himself to be
physician for all the world's weaknesses and sins. And
he can accomplish his end if he can make *whole* men out
of all these incomplete creatures with which the world is
filled:

> And God His glorious child shall know,
> His heir, the Adam that he wrought.

But if this is to take place, he has to take up the struggle against these three demons that are called light-heart,
faint-heart, and wild-heart, and to lay them low. And
here the first act ends, and here ends also the introduction or *exposition* of the drama.

The *complication* begins in Act II. And it begins long
before Brand dreams of any such possibility. For the
part which circumstances now force him to play is as
different from the part he had intended to play as darkness is from light. He soon has to learn that in order
to be the champion of the ideal, it is not enough to go
in triumphal procession through the world as the brilliant, irresistible preacher, but he must *sacrifice!* He
must let himself be plucked bare, to the last thread. His
whole roadway through life, as he expresses it, must be
"built upon sacrificial stones."

It so happens that a famine comes upon his native

village, and his people are changed almost into beasts.
Each one snatches everything upon which he can lay
hands, and does not care a whit what becomes of the
others who are starving. Einar at once begins to empty
his pockets, and would have given more if he had had
anything more to give. The Mayor sitting upon a pile
of provisions and doling out rations, gets a high opinion
of Einar but a very poor one of Brand. For he gives
nothing. He stands there silent and reserved to all ap-
pearances quite unmoved. In reality he is aflame with
the desire to pour forth gifts:

> Oh, if the blood of all my heart
> Could heal you from the hunger-smart,
> In welling streams it should be shed,
> Till every vein was a dry bed.
> But here it were a sin to give!

This famine is only a warning reprimand which God has
sent to draw men from the morass of materialism in
which they are mired:

> But men whom misery has not mann'd
> Are worthless of the saving hand!

And so he gives nothing, and this "flinty soul" comes
within an ace of being driven from the village "by knife
and stone."

This was Brand's first sacrifice. For, to be true to his
conviction, he had to sacrifice his burning desire to help
and also the thanks and homage of his native village.
This is a true foretaste of what his whole life holds in
store for him.

In the meantime, he does not have to wait long for
the second demand which is made upon him for sacrifice. As the villagers are about to drive Brand out of
the village, a woman comes, wild and dishevelled, in
deepest despair. Across the fjord her husband lies at
the point of death, and yet he *dares* not die. He has
slain his youngest child; for he could not bear to see it
starve to death. But at once he saw the horror of his
deed, proclaimed himself a murderer and turned the

knife upon himself so that he was wounded to death. The woman sought a pastor; but there was no pastor, for he had gone away at the first threats of famine. The fjord is in an uproar of wind and waves, so everyone says that it is impossible to cross over. Just to try would be to tempt Providence. But Brand is willing to give his life if someone will accompany him on the dire journey. For "here is need." But no one dares. Not even Einar. Yes, Agnes dares. Brand has already exercised over her so powerful an influence, has become so big to her that she fearlessly follows where he leads. And they cross in safety, as by a miracle. Brand speaks to the man, and he dies in peace.

This was the second sacrifice: he offers his life (or rather risks it, is *willing* to offer it) to save a man in need — in despair of soul.

But then representatives from the community come to Brand. They want him to be their pastor, for if they could get such a man to lead them, there might be hope of their betterment also. — Brand can hardly trust his own ears when they deliver the message. *He* a pastor in this inaccessible valley! And for these people! Thanks, no! That would be to forsake his high calling. But the spokesman for the party is not so easily turned aside. Upon Brand's assuring him that his calling is his "very life," the man replies with Brand's own statement earlier in the conversation:

> Though you give all and life retain,
> Remember, that your gift is vain.

And when Brand with dignity declares that there may be one exception:

> One thing is yours you may not spend:
> Your very inmost Self of all.
> You may not bind it, may not bend,
> Nor stem the river of your call.
> To make for ocean is its end,

the man answers:

> Though tarn and moorland held it fast, —
> As dew 'twould reach the sea at last.

Brand is surprised to hear such words from this man's lips, and he becomes thoughtful; nevertheless, he sends the men away with a determined refusal. But in his own mind he begins to waver and feel unsure of himself. — Then his eye falls upon Agnes, who sits in a wonderful trance. Since her meeting with Brand, a remarkable transformation has been taking place in her soul. And she is now witnessing this change in a vision of a world that is being created. When she in two of the most brilliant speeches in the play has recounted her vision to Brand, it begins to dawn upon him that it is not the ostentatious deed of heroism which is the greatest, as he until that very moment had imagined, but the quiet, unknown, unostentatious working, inward, into one's own and others' hearts. And so when he immediately thereafter meets his mother — assuredly the most earthbound materialist a poet has ever portrayed, not excepting even Shylock — he sees after a long talk with her, and after a bitter struggle with himself, that it really is his *duty*, his *call*, to remain in the valley. And thereby he makes a two-fold sacrifice; he gives up the world as his plane of activity for the narrow, sunless valley; and he gives up the glorious, ostentatious outward service before the eyes of men, for the quiet inward activity, hidden from common view, the work with the individual. This is Brand's third sacrifice.

Then Brand becomes pastor in the valley. And Agnes becomes his wife and the lone sunbeam in Brand's life and home, as well as in the whole valley; yes, one might almost say, the only ray of light in that dark and serious drama. But she is a sunbeam that shines with a marvellously clear ray.

Meanwhile, Brand gets into difficulties with the Mayor, the representative of officialdom in the valley. The Mayor soon discovers that two cocks are too many for one basket, and so he gives him the choice between leaving the village, and fighting his way against the

Mayor and his party.   Brand chooses the latter, — a
sacrifice once more.   He sacrifices the friendship of the
leaders, sacrifices the privilege of being "Caesar's
friend."

But on the very heels of this sacrifice follows the
fifth, and up to this time the hardest.   It was not least
of all for his mother's sake that Brand decided to remain in the valley.   He had to be near her, in order, if
possible, to save her soul.   He had promised her that
when she was in trouble and needed his help, she had
only to send him word, and he would come to her "ten-
der both as priest and child," come with song and words
of comfort, and with the Holy Sacrament.   But — only
on *one condition:* she must first give up all she owns, *all*,
even to the last clout.   Until that time, he neither could
nor dared to come; "clean board for the wine and bread
of grace."   That he is a very poor "curate of souls" is
apparent to everyone; but, as I have said before, Brand
was not intended to represent a "curate of souls."   Instead of visiting her and trying to help her free herself
from the trammels of the world, he goes his own way,
waiting for the message that she is free.   He has heard
that she is ill, — yes, dying, — and he waits with ever-
increasing suspense for the message.   But it does not
come.   Yes — at last.   But has she given up *all?*   No,
only half.   And again Brand goes and waits, and again
comes the messenger.   Now she is willing to give *all?*
No, only nine tenths.   Then comes the third message:
his mother is dead — dead impenitent.   He has sacrificed his mother's salvation, we might say, for what he
believed to be God's will, sacrificed, although he yearned
to save.

Then comes the sixth sacrifice: Brand must offer up
his only child, his little son Alv.   Both Brand and Agnes
worship this child with an almost idolatrous love; he is
the sunshine of their lives.   Then the doctor comes and
tells them that if they spend one more winter in the valley, they will have no little Alv when spring comes

again. But if they will go farther south, and go at once, they can assuredly save the child's life. And they decide to go — at once — indeed, that very day. Brand, in other words, is at the point of betraying his charge. But the doctor cannot forbear jeering a little at him, who is so merciless toward others and so lenient toward himself and his own. Then comes a member of the congregation and tells Brand that it is his *duty* to remain in the valley. His people cannot do without him: at any rate, *he*, the messenger, cannot, — and then Gerd appears again. She mocks the "preacher" (she means Brand) who, she says, has now gone away and has thus given complete freedom to the evil spirits to work in the valley. How she rejoices over their triumph! And when Brand reprimands her for trying to trick him with idolatrous songs, she points her finger at Alv and says, "Idols? Man, I show you one!"

And so Brand has to decide to stay — and to sacrifice his child. And Alv dies! This is the climax of the rising action.

This is the situation at the beginning of Act IV, or, technically speaking — at the beginning of the "falling action": Brand has sacrificed Alv, sacrificed all that he thought dearest and most indispensable to him in the world. But still he has Agnes, and in truth she is (as he later has to learn) even more indispensible to him than Alv, if he is to be able to continue to tend his pastoral charge there in the valley. For Agnes comes as close to ideal womanhood as a poet has ever been able to make one of his characters. Alv's death must have been even more bitter to her, the mother. But she does not utter a complaint — not so much as a single word — does not expostulate with God, who has been so cruel as to deprive her of her only child. But she must speak about Alv; be permitted to treasure his memory. It seems a comfort to her when she can busy herself with things that remind her of him — his clothes, for example. But Brand thinks this is idolatry. She *shall* not

mourn her loss. His heart is near to breaking when he
feels that he must tell her this, and we involuntarily
shudder even as we read it, and we cannot but think of
the contrast between Brand's attitude toward Agnes,
and the attitude of Jesus to the sorrow-laden, as f. ex.,
the widow of Nain. But Brand believes Agnes's attitude to be idolatry, and he thinks that he must "Shatter
her last idol shrine." And thus he is forced again and
again to stifle his tenderest feelings for the most dearly
beloved of God's creatures upon earth — in order not
to be disobedient to what he believes to be the will of
God.

Before this struggle is over, he is called upon to give
once more — a gift this time with which Brand can part
with comparative ease, but which for his mother (and
for many another) had been the hardest of all to give
up. Agnes has begun to hint that the *church* is too *small*,
and so he decides to give the rich inheritance which had
come to him upon the death of his mother for the building of a new church. That is, he strips himself completely of material wealth.

Then follows the last struggle to make Agnes part
with everything that reminds her of Alv. A gipsy
woman comes to the house with a half-frozen youngster,
and Brand demands of Agnes that she give this dis-
reputable stranger Alv's clothes — *all* of them. And
Agnes gives — at first unwillingly, then willingly, yes
gladly.

And now Agnes's sacrifices are at an end; but so also
is her life. Now she must die. Brand can still win her
back to life, she says, if he will. And she gives him the
choice between letting her bind herself to things of the
world, and thus risk losing her world (as in the matter
of the clothes), and sacrificing her life, reconciling himself to the thought of her leaving him: "At the cross-
way stand'st thou: choose!" And Brand chooses to
give her life.

AGNES.
Goodnight.
Thanks for all. Now I will rest.

[Goes.]

BRAND.
Soul, be patient in thy pain!
Triumph in its bitter cost.
All to lose was all to gain,
Nought abideth but the Lost!

Then the day for the dedication of the new church
arrives. And again Brand clashes with officialdom,
especially with the Dean, the representative of higher
ecclesiastical authority. And now they completely take
away his breath. They have secured a royal decora-
tion for him, but before he is knighted, the Dean wants
him to be a good boy and agree to certain conditions
which, says the Dean, are, of course, so self-evident
that they scarcely need to be mentioned, but which he
wants to state in order to make sure that all parties are
clear on the matter. As a pastor in the established
church, Brand must consider himself first and foremost
a servant of the state, and the church he has built a gift
to the state:

This church, you see, you have conferred
Upon the State, for its sole profit;
And, therefore, all the uses of it
Must to the State's advantage tend.
This is the meaning, note it well,
Of our forthcoming celebration,
This shall be meant by chiming bell,
And this by Gift-deed's recitation.

So says the Dean. And when Brand calls God to witness that such was never his intention and that he will
never agree to any such conditions, the Dean informs
him that it is now too late. But the Dean "must almost
laugh" at such a fuss about a trifle:

What is the tragedy therein?
You are not asked to promise sin?
Souls do not grow more hard to save
Because the Country profits too;

With due discretion and despatch
Two masters' bidding you may do;
You were not made a priest, to snatch
Peter or Harry's single soul
Out of the torments of the lake;
But that the parish as a whole
Might of the shower of grace partake;
And the whole Parish saved, it's clear
You save every Parishioner.

Brand finds that of all the blind moles, of all the
stupid philistines he has met in the valley, the Dean is
the worst.   I suppose the Dean is intended to represent
the worldly mass within the established church.   But
immediately after this encounter, Brand meets Einar,
who has become very religious, yes, even a missionary.
He seems to be very zealous in the cause of the Lord,
but it is soon apparent that his specialty is to judge —
to judge everyone and everything — except himself.
Einar is a caricature of the pietist.   In him also, Brand
fails to find understanding and sympathy.

And so it becomes evident to Brand that he can no
longer serve as pastor in the valley.   But not only that:
he must get away, away from all this church politics,
away from the established church.   And as the officials,
both great and small, and the whole festal host are waiting for the church to be opened, Brand strides to the
door, locks it, and throws the key into the fjord.   And
so Brand again makes a sacrifice: he gives up his position in the church, which in this case means that he has
outlawed himself from both church and society.

But has not Brand betrayed his charge, his *call* which
he has hitherto declared sovereign, and for which he has
sacrificed so much?   No, not his *call*, only his *position*
in a church which he can no longer accept as the true
church, but only as a caricature of it.   He is going to
establish a new congregation, "fair and free," and as
pastor for this group he will go out into the world and
work for the true church, God's church, God's kingdom

on earth. He cries out to the holiday-clad multitude:

> Oh, it was not to this end
> That the offering cup I drained.
> .   .   .   .
> It [the church] has neither mark nor bound,
> And its floor the green earth is,
> Mead and mountain, sea and sound;
> And the overarching sky
> Is its only canopy.
> There shall all thy work be wrought
> As an anthem for God's ear,
> There thy week-day toil be sought
> With no sacrilege to fear.
> There the world be like a tree
> Folded in its shielding bark;
> Faith and Action blended be.
> There shall daily labor fuse
> With right Teaching and right Use,
> Daily drudgery be one
> With star-flights beyond the sun,
> One with Yule-tide revelry
> And the Dance before the Ark.

In brief: The Church or God's Kingdom shall en-
compass the whole world. Everything that we do shall
be done to the glory of God. The Church shall conse-
crate all of life.

Then he calls to the multitude and invites them to
follow him and found such a church:

> Come, thou young man, fresh and free,
> Let a life-breeze lighten thee
> From this dim vault's clinging dust.
> Conquer with me! . . .
> Over frozen height and hollow,
> Over all the land we'll fare,
> Loose each soul-destroying snare
> That this people holds in fee,
> Lift and lighten and set free,
> Blot the vestige of the beast,
> Each a Man, and each a Priest,
> Stamp anew the outworn brand,
> Make a Temple of the land.

And the multitude follows him. Only a few remain
behind. The Mayor and the Dean and those few do

what they can to stop them; but far away they hear
voices:

> Ours they are not if they quail! . .
> Be against us, or be for us!

And so up over the moorlands bears their course.

Now what are we to think about this performance?
Are we to believe that out of that horde it will be possible for Brand to build the new congregation, which is
to recreate and spread God's kingdom over the whole
earth? What are we to think about this "multitude"?
Have their eyes been opened to a vision of the ideal?
Have they recognized the absolute validity of the "ideal
demand," so that they are now, like Brand, willing to
sacrifice everything for what they acknowledge to be
God's will? No, indeed, we have no such opinion. Nor
has Ibsen given us the slightest reason for forming such
an opinion. If we follow the course of events during
this festival, we shall soon see that it is not the urge to
do God's will, whatever the cost, which drives these
people to action. It is the intoxication of the moment.
They are moved by the spirit of the festival. At best
we can ascribe to them the objective which Brand later
names:

> Through all bosoms thrill'd the longing
> For a greater Day's dawn-light;
> . . . .
> But the sacrifice they dread!
> Will, the weakling, hides his head.

So now we know that Brand will not be successful in
his undertaking to recreate a kingdom of God. In fact,
we know more than that. We know that if every crea-
ture in this multitude were on the same plane as Brand
with respect to an understanding of the "ideal demand"
and a willingness to sacrifice, he could not have been
successful. We know that even Brand lacks the basic
requisite for such a performance. But concerning that
we shall say nothing further at this point, because it be-

comes apparent only in the last episode of the story, in the closing lines of the play.

But here we have reached the most vital point of the play, as far as its main purpose is concerned. For just here we can see the great abyss that yawns between such a man as Brand, who wills completely what he knows to be God's will, and who does not shrink from any sacrifice necessary to put him on good footing with Our Lord, — between such a man, I say, and the common earthbound soul, for whom it is not of the greatest importance to please God and his own conscience, and thus to keep on a good footing with Our Lord.

And we are soon given an opportunity to see this cleavage. A little weariness, a little hunger, a little foot-soreness — and their enthusiasm is dampened, their longing for "a greater Day's dawn-light" is gone. Then they go willingly and meekly back to their life in the valley, back to their old leaders, whom they have so recently accused of leading them astray. It was the idea of sacrifice that affrighted them.

But before the people go back into the valley, leaving Brand standing alone and forsaken up there on the cold and barren moors, another bitter sacrifice is demanded of him. When the crowd has followed him a short distance and it is getting late, they give Brand to understand that if he expects them to follow him farther, he will have to make clear a few matters which were not explained before they started off:

> Firstly, how long we shall make war.
> Then, of our total loss therein.
> And finally, — how much we win.

In other words, how long the struggle is going to last, how much they are going to have to sacrifice of what is dear to them, and finally, how much they are personally going to get out of it.

It isn't easy to be Brand at the moment. If he now is true to the watchword he himself has followed, "All

or nothing," it is clear that not a single person will follow him a step farther. He will be left alone, a pastor
without a parish, forsaken, apparently, by both God
and man. Surely he must moderate the demand. But
no, — here is his answer:

> How long the war will last?
> As long as life, till ye have cast
> All ye possess before the Lord,
> And slain the Spirit of Accord;
> Until your stiff will bend and bow,
> And every coward scruple fall
> Before the bidding: Nought or All!
> What you will lose? Your gods abhorr'd,
> Your feasts to Mammon and the Lord,
> The glittering bonds ye do not loathe,
> And all the pillows of your sloth!
> What you will gain? A will that's whole,
> A soaring faith, a single soul,
> The willingness to lose that gave
> Itself rejoicing to the grave; —
> A crown of thorns on every brow; —
> That is the wage you're earning now.

Then there is trouble. They cry, "Betrayed, betrayed! Deceived! Misled!" And the Mayor and the
Dean just at that moment join the group and conduct
themselves affably toward the people, speaking to them
mildly and in friendly wise without the slightest hint
about anything like sacrifice, but with promises of full
forgiveness for all the pain and trouble they have caused
their officials and *real* guides, promises of a life of continued peace and quiet down in the valley. And as
they, to cap the climax, tell them a falsehood about a
shoal of a million fish which has just entered the fjord,
the mob turns with defiant roars upon Brand, shouting:

> Hoo, never heed him! Stone and knife!
> Send the fiend flying for his life!

Brand is driven with stones out into the wilds, and the
mob returns to the valley below.

Brand is alone up on the barren moor. Another fearful defeat! Another fearful sacrifice, the hardest of all

— and the last? No, neither the hardest nor the last. Two more are yet to be required of him, each harder than the preceding.

As Brand, bleeding and broken, sits on a stone up there weeping softly and moaning,

> Alv and Agnes, come to me!
> Lone I sit upon this peak!
> Keen the north wind pierces through me,
> Phantoms seize me, chill ones, meek — !

he looks up, and sees "a glimmering space open and clear in the mist; the Apparition of a Woman stands in it, brightly clad" and opens its arms to him. It is Agnes. She tells him that all the agony through which he has gone is nothing but an illusion, "fever'd dreams."

> Dear, by sickness thou wast wasted, —
> Frenzy's bitter hast thou tasted,
> Dreamt thy wife had fled afar.

But she is alive, and so also is little Alv, "with unfaded brow"; and all that he has sacrificed, or thought that he sacrificed, will come back to him, and all will be joy and peace.

> Brand, be kind; my heart is warm;
> Clasp me close in thy strong arm;
> Let us fly where summer's sun —

Yes, he can have all of it once more, but only on one condition: he must be a little more compliant and sensible, a little more humane, and must blot out three little words, "All or Nought." But if he is unwilling, the darkness of night must still hover over him, and in that night there will not be the faintest glimmering of hope ever to triumph, for:

> One with fiery-sword of yore
> Man of Paradise bereft!
> At the gate a gulf he cleft; —
> Over that thou mayst not soar!

To this Brand replies:

> But the path of yearning's left.

Which is to say: rather than lower my ideal and become

dull and stupid like the valley folk, I will go forward even though I may never be victorious and win my way to Paradise. But I may still yearn — yearn for Paradise, yearn to be in complete harmony with the ideal, with God's will. And then it can't be helped if I again must lose you and Alv, and all else which I before have sacrificed.

But what does this reply signify? It signifies that Brand once more must give up everything! The greatness of it is overwhelming, especially when we remember Brand's condition at the time. *He sacrifices everything a second time!*

And here Ibsen might easily have let the avalanche descend and the curtain fall. For here he has really completed the exposition of the main theme of the play. Here is the catastrophe: the Apparition — that is to say, the "spirit of compromise" vanishes in a thunderclap with the cry: "Die! Earth cannot use thee more!" and Brand stands there triumphant over the temptations of the spirit, — stands like one who has suffered the most crushing defeat, and yet like a conqueror — conqueror of that against which he has in all this drama struggled, the spirit of compromise. Or, in other words: in this work Ibsen, as before remarked, has wished to show the enormous difference between the man who *wills*, and the dull horde which lacks willpower; between the man who sees the "ideal demand," acknowledges its absolute validity, and is willing to give his all to meet that demand, and the dull horde which cannot see this ideal steadily (although they may catch occasional brief glimpses of it), neither acknowledge its validity, nor will sacrifice much for its attainment — only a little now and then, never *all;* between the man for whom the most important thing in life is to do God's will as he understands it, and the dull horde which find almost everything else more important, and first and foremost the avoidance of bringing any great sacrifice.

And now we can understand why the pastor Brand

would have been impossible as the exponent of the theme if he had been a real — not to say model — curate of souls. It is not within the scope of the play to show what the grace of God can effect in an individual or what a person can accomplish under the influence of God's love.

Then follows the question: Of what value to Brand are all his struggles? In what sense was he better off than the others there in the valley? I purposely use the word *value*. For assuredly we know that the ideal state is to do good for its own sake, without asking about other values. It is "value" enough, one might say, that at the close he still stood forth, strong and courageous, conqueror over the "spirit of compromise," stood there like a giant amongst mannikins and dwarfs. Surely, but I mean "value" for eternity, "value" in the sense that we Christians speak of it in connection with the soul's salvation. Yes, in this sense also one may say that the value of his experience was great. And this it is which is suggested in the closing episode, — merely suggested. It is so briefly referred to, this great change which finally takes place in Brand. But it seems that Ibsen could not bring the drama to a close without the suggestion. Was it perhaps to avoid the accusation that he taught that a man could save himself, if his will-power is sufficiently strong?

It is just this situation which makes matters so difficult for many a reader, and not least of all for the scholarly critic. It is as though Ibsen suddenly tried to discredit the very idea which he has emphasized so strongly before. In all the preceding is echoed and re-echoed, "It is the will which counts." Here at the close Brand asks,

> Shall they wholly miss thy Light
> Who unto man's utmost might
> Will'd — ?

So often the reader cannot — or will not — see that Ibsen is here speaking of something entirely different: not about the ethical, but about the religious; about salvation, in the religious sense. In the preceding part of the play, Ibsen has been trying to show a man who is uncompromising in morals. In the concluding lines, he suggests that not even the strongest iron will counts for much in the matter of salvation. Indeed, this is a weakness from the point of view of dramatic conception and unity; but I wonder if one should not be grateful to Ibsen nevertheless for adding it? It is assuredly one of the most sublime passages that Ibsen has written. And if anyone objects that Ibsen was too great a dramatic artist to permit himself such a flaw in dramatic technique, what shall we say of a ghost scene in a historical play (*The Pretenders*)? And, again, if one raises the objection that such a Christian point of view was not Ibsen's, even when he wrote *Brand*, what will they say about the conclusion to *The Pretenders* and *Peer Gynt?*

When Brand has put the "hawk" or the "spirit of compromise" to flight, Gerd puts in an appearance once more. She too has waged a constant warfare with the hawk, has striven early and late to get him within range, so that she can put an end to him. Not for the same reason as Brand: in order completely and perfectly to do God's will; no, but in order completely to follow her own will, completely to do as she pleases, to be free from all responsibility to society, to the church, to all and everything — except her own desires. Gerd and Brand are basically two of a kind: what they do, they do completely and whole-heartedly. But Brand becomes tamed (civilized); his will becomes subject to ethical demands. Gerd is still wild, untamed. And like the unbroken horse, she will not endure either bridle or reins. Now she comes to him once more, and when she sees how badly the people for whom Brand worked so hard have treated him, that he is lame and blood-stained, and especially that he weeps, then the ice is gone from her heart; then she is so completely lost in wonder and awe for this man that she thinks he is the "savior," and wants to fall down and worship him.

> I know thee now! . . .
> The One, greatest Man art thou!

Brand replies:

> So I madly dared to trust.

Had he not at the beginning let it be known that he was the physician of humanity?

That this error of Gerd's is intended as the greatest of Brand's temptations is apparent both from his reply, and (more especially) from the manner in which he greets Gerd's attempt at worshipping him: "Get thee hence!" he cries, as Jesus had said to the tempter in the wilderness. But now is also the heart of Brand warmed; now he brings his last great gift: his selfrighteousness. Now he falls upon his knees and confesses:

> Oh, no saving plank I see,
> In my own soul's agony!

Now he confesses that he is the "meanest worm that crawls," and that he stands but at "the first step of the ascent." That is to say: all that I have done, all that I have sacrificed, has not brought me so far even as upon the first step of the ladder which leads to salvation, to heaven. It has all in the deepest sense been valueless in the sight of God when it comes to a question of God, when it comes to a question of *earning* salvation. All he has done, all he has sacrificed, has not been pleasing in the sight of God. And why not? What has been lacking? It is *love* which has been lacking, love of God, true love, has not been the motivating influence in a single one of Brand's good deeds. And consequently, from the religious point of view, all of his work is valueless. All he has done has in the final analysis been done for himself, to win a place for himself in God's esteem — not willingly, not driven by love, but often with clenched teeth, against his wish, yes, contrary to his *will* — because he had to and *would* meet the demand laid upon

him to act the *man*. And he has become a strong man
— but not a Christian. Now at last he humbled himself. Now he can pray:

> Of salvation's vesture, stain'd
> With the wine of tears unfeign'd
> Let me clasp one fold at last!

Now his refrain is:

> From today my life shall stream
> Lambent, glowing, as a dream.
> The ice-fetters break away,
> I can weep, — and kneel, — and pray!

Now at last is Ibsen through with Brand. And now
the avalanche comes. In answer to Brand's question,

> Shall they wholly miss thy Light
> Who unto Man's utmost might
> Will'd — ?

the answer comes,

> God is *deus caritatis* (the God of love).

The only natural explanation of this answer, as given in
this particular connection, must be that in the matter
of Salvation, one must *begin* with love, God's love to
the sinner; in other words, not "First the will," as you,
Brand, have always insisted.

Just what part human will plays in this connection is
not explained. As we have observed, it was not unim-
portant in the case of Brand. It did bring him to the
first step of the stair of salvation, to the realization that
he needed a Savior. We cannot see that any of the
valley folk got so far — except Gerd.

If this explanation of *Brand* is correct — and re-
peated reading and study have not suggested to me any
other possible explanation — in the main, at least, when
one keeps strictly to the text of the play — it is to be
hoped that we can give answers to the questions suggested above. It is surely evident that in this play, at
least, Ibsen has not proclaimed atheistic ideas, but has

based his whole theme on fundamentally Christian
principles. And I believe we can also agree that Ibsen
has here proved himself a great poet and dramatist. But
is he not also a great moral teacher? Not of *new*
Ibsenish ideas. That the law demands all, that one
who walks the way of the law must go in for self-denial
and sacrifice, that one by the way of the law cannot
ascend even the first step in the ladder of salvation, etc.,
— all of these are well-known ideas. They are taken
from the Bible. Nevertheless, is not Ibsen a teacher?
Do we not get the impression that Ibsen was much concerned about impressing these ideas upon his readers?
And if that is the case, then surely he is a teacher.

But in the reading of Brand there are myriads of
other questions constantly cropping up, and some of
them may possibly not be so easy to answer. For example, about the plausibility of such characters as Brand
and Agnes: Is it possible for a human being by his
own might to go so far in self-denial and sacrifice as
Brand and Agnes? As far as Agnes is concerned, we
see at all times that it is not exclusively by her own will
and power that she dedicates herself to death. Even
before she becomes Brand's wife, we hear these words
from her lips:

> And I rather feel than see
> Him who sits enthroned above,
> Feel that He looks down on me
> Full of sadness and of love,
> Tender-bright as morning's breath,
> And yet sorrowing unto death.

And Brand is to blame for her not getting before the
very end a clear conception of God as a *father*. She often
begs Brand to look upon God more as a kind father
than as a stern judge.

As for Brand, it is clear as day that until the very
last meeting with Gerd, he looks upon God as the re-
lentless taskmaster who demands and demands; and as
soon as a vestige of the father-aspect tries to make its
appearance, Brand carefully conceals it.

Is he plausible? That is a difficult question to answer. We are often surprised at what even a heathen will do to satisfy the demands of his stern god. Read the history of missions. It is full of the most, one might say, unbelievable instances. Or better still, read the story of Luther in the days before he found peace. I wonder if there is any sacrifice which he would have thought too great to give in return for peace?

And yet it will be hard to find a parallel to what Brand does, when everything is taken into consideration. First he deprives himself of everything that he holds dear, absolutely everything; and then, when finally he is stoned and hounded away by those for whom he has made the sacrifice, and the promise comes to him that he shall have all restored to him and with Agnes "seek sunshine and summer" if he will but moderate the program of action which has brought him to this sad pass, he answers that he must continue in the same way as he began, then indeed he seems to be doing more than is possible for one who is untouched by

> Salvation's vesture stain'd
> With the wine of tears unfeign'd.

It has therefore often occurred to me that if this powerful drama suffers from any weakness, it must be this that the hero as a human being is too strong. But in his capacity of teacher and doer of the Law, he cannot be too strong.

But why Ibsen now and then lets Brand go beyond the Law, and demand more than God himself, it is impossible to explain satisfactorily. But that is just what he does when he tortures Agnes to death with accusations of idolatry. If we read this portion of the work with care, I think we shall agree that at first there was in her relation to Alv and the things that reminded her of him not the slightest suggestion of idol worship. One could hardly call her a natural *mother* had she not mourned him thus. That Alv's clothes for a time at

least, become more precious to her than all else — for
that we have Brand to blame. He practically drives her
to idolatrous practices by the picture of God which he
constantly keeps before her. And never is Agnes
greater than when she comes victorious out of the conflict, and sees clearly the father-countenance of God that
she always has wanted to look upon.

*   *   *   *

Well, these are just a few of the questions that sug-
gest themselves to the reader of *Brand;* we should not
soon finish our task if we tried to discuss *all* of them.
Neither was that my intention in this study, which was
for the most part originally prepared as a summarizing
lecture for a class in Norwegian literature which had
just completed the reading of *Brand.* Whether it really
belongs in a theological journal I have my doubts;
but that is for others to decide: it is by the request of
the editor that I submit it. But if it helps in any way
to shed light upon the plan and purpose of *Brand,*
which to many persons is Ibsen's most obscure drama,
and if it gives a few suggestions as to how Ibsen ought
to be read, it cannot perhaps be said to be entirely out of
place. For whatever one may think about Ibsen, he *was*
a great poet — about that there cannot be the slightest
doubt. He has wielded great influence, and will continue increasingly to do so. And he was a *Norwegian*
poet, in many respects the greatest Norway has produced, and certainly her most famous.

The PILLARS OF SOCIETY
Translated by Olav Lee

THE PILLARS OF SOCIETY

Between *Brand* and *Peer Gynt* on one side, and *The Pillars of Society* on the other, the distance chronologically is, to be sure, not very great. *Brand* was published in 1866, *Peer Gynt* in 1867, and *The Pillars of Society* in 1877, and so the distance between the first two dramas mentioned and the last one was only eleven and ten years respectively. But the distance between these dramas considered with reference to the history of literature appears like a yawning "Ginungagap." When *Brand* and *Peer Gynt* were published, romanticism was still the dominant influence — in Norwegian literature, at any rate; when *The Pillars of Society* was published, romanticism and even the faintest breath of it had long since been renounced. Literary tendency had passed through the period of realism and far into that of naturalism, which is its consequent continuation and fruit. Traveling is often done by means of seven-league boots in the realm of the spirit, just as it is in the fairy tale.

For a time very rapid strides had been made. There had been a descent from the sunny summits of romanticism, from a world such as one dreamed that it was and as one wished it to be, to a world such as it really was or as one supposed it to be. As romanticism had seen or had wished to see only the sunny side of existence, so naturalism wished to see little else than its shady side. Is it possible to conceive of a greater contrast with respect to the view of life? Romanticism sees in the entire existence an outflowing of divine love: God is in everything, in the least as well as in the greatest. We are exhorted

> To sense the high
> In nature's eye,
> Adoring sight
> The Godhead's light
> In sun and violet,
> In small things and in great.

For it is God who directs everything, both great and small. The motive power and the fundamental principle in all existence is the love of God. He has a purpose behind everything that comes to pass, and He will manage all for the best.

Naturalism regards all existence as nature or as the product of nature, and as that only. The world has in some way come into existence, and is of such and such a character. Why? That we do not know. And what is the motive power or fundamental principle in life? Egoism, and that only, — the struggle for existence, resulting in the survival of the fittest. There is no consciousness of God or of divine love. But what caused this violent change of view, this reversal? A large book might be written in answer to that question. We shall only mention a few of the most important causes.

The attitude of romanticism is, as one may see, mainly the Biblical one, with this difference that the Bible does not forget to mention the dark side of life — man's corruptness and obstinacy, which so often hinder God from carrying out his benevolent purposes. Romanticism did not deny anything in the Bible. Far from it. But it did not like to dwell on the darker aspects of life. In that realm it was afraid of the light: although it viewed with pleasure the bright aspects of life, it did not suffer light to be shed on those that are dark and disgusting. Life as it appears in this noisy machine age, especially in the cities, was something which romanticism wished neither to see nor depict. But the idyllic country life, resounding with *lur* and cow-bells, the warbling of birds, the roar of waterfalls, enlivened by nix, *hulder*, elf, and brownie; and, above all, the sturdy, dependable, unsophisticated farmer and his patriarchal family life — these romanticism loved to see and to portray, especially when viewed in the distant past, for the past was more to its liking than the present. And it showed a special predilection for the Middle Ages, the time when imagination and emotion were particularly

active: for romanticism was an imaginative and emotional tendency. It had, to be sure, started as a reaction
against an older tendency, the idealizing of reason and
culture in the "era of enlightenment." And then romanticism had gone to just as great extremes in one
direction as the "era of enlightenment" had gone in the
other.

And not only in polite literature did romanticism hold
sway. Natural philosophy was saturated with it. Nature was viewed from a romantic standpoint, and history and historical composition were colored by romanticism. In short, romanticism reigned supreme. Even
in politics, the most unromantic of all activities, romanticism had found entrance. A striking example of this
appears in what was done at the constitutional conven-
tion at Eidsvold in the year 1814. The great majority
in that assembly consisted of government officials. And
yet, because of their passion for the Saga period and the
Norse peasants, they with enthusiasm placed the political power in the hands of the farmers, — a power
which the officials had hitherto possessed almost exclusively and which they, as it appeared only a few
years later, had no intention whatever of giving up.

In the first half of the 19th century a childish optimism made people believe that the leading principle in
politics was chivalry or altruism and that the surest
guaranty which the smaller states had for their liberty
and independence was the great states, — the very ones
which in every age have shown themselves to be the
most hostile and dangerous enemies of the small states.
This was the condition from about 1800 to about 1850.

A reaction was inevitable. It had secretly been grow-
ing for a long time before it came out in the open. The
men who especially had been the pioneers of the
new tendency were following the French philosopher
Auguste Compte, the English scientist Charles Darwin,
the philosopher Herbert Spencer, the French author of

the history of English literature, Hippolyte Taine, and
the Danish Jew and literary critic, Georg Brandes.

Auguste Compte did not wish to dream or to specu-
late; his only desire was to see how the different phenomena of existence appear. He makes a clear distinction between the various stages of development: the
theological, the metaphysical, and the scientific. As
long as the primitive or theological stage was the accepted one, a common saying was: "Behind every phenomenon stands a divinity." When the metaphysical
stage was reached, the saying became: "Behind every
phenomenon there is a law." But since the third or
scientific stage has been reached, we are told that the
correct view is: "Such are the phenomena. Why? We
do not know."

Next comes Darwin with his "struggle for existence"
and with it his doctrine of "survival of the fittest." And
thus the motive power in existence, the basic principle,
has become egoism in its most crass form, and not love
as heretofore.

And now everything has become natural science;
Herbert Spencer applies the Darwinian theory to human
society. The history and development of a nation becomes a product of nature, like a birch tree or a kernel
of wheat: just as a birch from a small beginning ac-
quires its organs as they are needed, so also does human
society. In the beginning every man was warrior, fisherman, hunter, tailor, carpenter, and so forth. Nowa-
days several kinds of craftsmen are needed in the production of goods used in the making of one garment,
such as spinners, dyers, weavers, etc. That the Jews
differed from the Greeks, and the Greeks from the Ro-
mans, is dependent on blind natural laws and accidental
circumstances, such as heredity, environment, occupa-
tion, — all of them products of nature. Neither God
nor any divine instrumentality is necessary, — nothing
but nature.

Then Taine appears in the realm of literature. Now

every work of literature is said to be a product of nature,
a kind of "oyster-shell in which once a living organism
was found." The organism is there no longer, but by
studying its work we may learn to know it, and also to
know all the circumstances which have enabled this organism to produce the work. Take the work of Shakespeare, for example. From it we learn to know not only
Shakespeare himself, but his forbears, his cultural background, and the times and conditions in which he lived.
Why? Because all these things have been instrumental
in producing this work. According to this naturalistic
view, there is no place for any special poetic gift or inspiration. In other words, poetry is a product of nature.

Georg Brandes was the one who championed the
ideas of Taine in Northern Europe. When after a
lengthy stay in Paris he returned to Copenhagen in
1871, he had much to say, and was fully capable of saying it. Saturated with the ideas of Taine, he began
at once to agitate for their acceptance. And he was
just the kind of man who could agitate effectively. He
was a man of keen intellect, an enthusiastic proponent
of the new ideas, and a captivating orator. He delivered
a course of lectures at the University of Copenhagen,
in which he attacked Danish literature as it was and as
it had been for a long time.

It was the general opinion that Danish literature had
been enjoying its "golden age" since Oehlenschlæger
had appeared in 1802, and that it had never flourished
as it did under romanticism. But this could not frighten
Brandes from his view. Though admitting that romanticism might have some points in its favor, he maintained that it was an enemy of freedom and that therefore it was doomed, since freedom was the greatest of
all: personal liberty, the completest freedom in every
sense. The poet should be free to write about anything
and in whatever manner he saw fit. Only thus could a
literature of value arise, a vital literature. But in order
that such a literature might be possible, society as a

whole would have to be recast. "A new generation," he says, "must alter its whole conception of social relations; it must plough and rework the ground before a new literature can sprout." And so the poets would have to bestir themselves, and not lazily be dreaming, nor frittering their time away with art and the beautiful and such-like, nor singing about the nix and the hulder. On the contrary, they were to be reformers of society, to raise problems for discussion, to give a description of society exactly as it is, and to do this freely, courageously, and without circumlocution, neither to conceal nor to embellish anything, however ugly it may be. And they were also to point out how things ought to be: that would cause a revolution in the people's minds, and with it a new view and a new society. Literature would show that it was alive by recognizing the problems of the day, just as the French literature had begun to do. Among these problems which ought to be investigated and scrutinized in order to prove whether they were of any value, Brandes would include everything established or conventional: family life, marriage, and even religion (and not least that, for he seems to have regarded religion as a source of all evil).

This was then what Brandes and his naturalism offered as a program for the poet. It is easy to see what literature written according to these precepts would be in several important respects: 1. It would be godless. This it also became. We may safely say that infidelity in the seventies and eighties in all civilized countries had no greater or more effective advocate than the polite literature. 2. It would be cheerless, gloomy, and disconsolate. For it is not especially comforting to think that egoism is the basic principle of existence. 3. It would be ugly. In many instances it had to be what later in Norway was called "swine-literature."

We must, however, not forget to mention that this naturalistic literature had one saving trait — a trait of such beauty, nobility, and significance that one would be inclined to say that it has atoned for many of the great and numerous faults of this naturalistic tendency. Naturalism almost always takes cause with the weak, the oppressed, and the poor. Alexander Kjelland, who was a genuine naturalist, has as no one else in Norway scourged the great, the rich, and the mighty, although he belonged to one of the most aristocratic families and had been reared in a home of luxury and wealth.

Another thing which must not be forgotten is that it was possible for a writer to belong to the naturalistic group only as far as method is concerned; that is to say, one might depict life just as it is without being an infidel, or a pessimist, or a writer of the so-called "swine-literature." Jonas Lie is a striking example. I know of no Norwegian writer who has depicted life with such true realism as he, and he was neither a freethinker nor a pessimist; and he has not written a line that may not be read to any audience whatever. I dare not express any judgment as to the final religious attitude of Ibsen. It will, however, be difficult to point to anything in his work which necessarily must be construed as being irreligious or anti-Christian. With regard to the present he was a pessimist, but he was a pronounced optimist as regards the future. And his works may be read to any cultured gathering — yes, even *Ghosts!*

The program which naturalism placed before the poet was to prove everything established by custom, to discuss it thoroughly in order to find out whether it was of any value, and if it proved not to be, to replace it by something better; he was to depict everything, and neither conceal nor embellish the truth. This was the program placed before the writers of the North by Georg Brandes upon his return from Paris in 1871. Some European countries had been following it for a long time. In the Scandinavian countries, however, the acceptance of it was delayed; romanticism had reached the North much later than other countries, and there it stayed longer. To Denmark romanticism had come with the publication of Oehlenschlæger's *The Golden Horns* as early as 1802. In Norway it did not gain full admittance until 1842. But even in Norway romanticism may be said to have lost its sway by the close of the fifties. *The Sheriff's Daughters* by Camilla Collett, published in 1855, is not romantic, but realistic. Bjørnson's *Synnöve Solbakken* (1856) is more realistic than romantic; so also his stories *Arne* and *A Happy Boy*. Ibsen was but a short time under the sway of romanticism. In *The Comedy of Love* (1862) romanticism is more evident in the metrical form than in the contents. And in *The Pretenders* (1864) the only portion which may be classified as romantic is the ghost scene. In *Brand* (1866) and *Peer Gynt* (1867) he is combating romanticism, laying upon it the blame for nearly all the faults which he found in the Norwegian people. As early as 1869, two years before Brandes came home from Paris, he published his first fully realistic work, *The League of Youth*. Realism had shown itself still earlier in England. Dickens, Thackeray, and George Eliot are as realistic as anyone might wish, but naturalistic they are not.

During about twenty years naturalism had kept on making its way under the name of realism, a period which may be designated as naturalism's years of childhood and youth. For only when realism has reached its full development is it called naturalism. Then it became evident with what this new tendency was fraught. The ideas of Compte, Darwin, Spencer, and Taine had now unfolded themselves sufficiently to show their consequences.

In 1877 Norwegian literature received its first naturalistic work, *The Pillars of Society*. Whether Ibsen in this drama fully adheres to the naturalistic program we shall, I think, be able to tell by considering the contents and the plan of the work.

Contents and Plan of The Pillars of Society.

Owing to the many sub-plots which Ibsen has given this play to shed light on the main action, the presentation of the contents and the plan of this work must, unfortunately, be more lengthy than one might wish. In this play Ibsen follows, for the last time, the Shakespearian plan, with the traditional five acts clearly defined: Exposition, Rising Action, Climax, Falling Action, Catastrophe.

I. The Exposition. Act I.

The whole action takes place in the home of Consul Bernick, the town's most prominent citizen. He is a ship owner, and in company with the merchants Rummel, Vigeland, and Sandstad he manages a dockyard and other concerns. We are at first brought into his spacious garden-pavilion, where the "Society for the Morally Depraved" is just having a meeting. Every one of the ladies is busily occupied with her needlework. Rector Rørlund is seated at the end of the table. He is reading a story which the ladies find to be "highly instructive" and besides, "so very moral." While this is going on Shipbuilder Aune enters. He wishes to speak with the Consul. Mrs. Bernick points to the door of the Consul's office, but in the doorway Aune is met by the Consul's manager, Krap, who tells him that the Consul cannot see him to-day, and that he insists that Aune cease giving lectures to the workmen every Saturday, for they tend to disrupt society. "My society is not that of the Consul, sir," Aune angrily replies. Then Krap reminds Aune that his "society" is first and foremost the firm of Consul Bernick; "for that is our means of subsistence." And Aune leaves.

During this muffled conversation between Aune and Krap, Rector Rørlund has finished his reading. The story must have described something exceedingly beautiful that has occurred either in the city or elsewhere in Norway, for now they begin — and especially Rector

Rørund — to deem themselves indescribably fortun-
ate, because they are dwelling in a small community and not in one of those corrupt large communities
where all those monstrous things about which one daily
hears and reads are taking place, and of which they now
have such a dreadful example in the profligate American sailors who have been staying in town, waiting for
the time when their ship, the *Indian Girl*, will be ready
to sail.

Two of the ladies do not concur in the vociferous enthusiasm for the small communities and in the unspeakable dread of the large ones. These are the young Miss
Dina Dorf and Miss Martha Bernick, the Consul's sister. Dina Dorf has the audacity even to ask if there
are not "many great deeds" done in the great communities. The other ladies are struck almost speechless with
astonishment at such ignorance and such want of tact.
"No, dear Dina, it would not be well if such 'great things'
should gain entrance among us," the Rector said. "It
is of the greatest importance that our community be
kept unsullied by all this untried stuff which an impa-
tient age would force upon us." He continues by saying that they have reason to thank God that they have
succeeded in this, and especially have they reason to re-
joice that Consul Bernick last year as "an instrument
of Providence" succeeded in keeping out that railway
line which many were so insistent upon having. And
he seriously rebukes Miss Bernick, who although she
is a teacher has been so imprudent as to say that she
often, while in her schoolroom, could wish that she
"was far out on the wild ocean." That is merely a
temptation that must be banished, says Rector Rørlund.

From within the Consul's office loud talking is heard.
At the same moment Hilmar Tønnesen, Mrs. Bernick's
cousin, rushes breathlessly in and wants to know about
the meeting which he has heard that Consul Bernick is
now calling. He has heard that "this railway non-

sense" is again to be the subject of discussion. The others become quite frightened by this news. Hilmar, however, is of the opinion that it would be well if they might have some wrangling and hubbub again, to put spice into this tiresome village life. Hilmar who in his own estimation is a great hero, is in reality the greatest coward portrayed by Ibsen. He is frightened if only he hears a loud conversation; yet he believes that his vocation is to go about and "lift high the banner of the ideal," especially when heroic action is required. Because of this he often makes fun of little Olaf, the Consul's son, for being afraid — which Olaf is not.

Mrs. Holt, a member of the society, is a comparatively recent citizen of this town, and since the rest of the members have emphasized that conditions are a great deal better now than formerly, she wants to know why former conditions were so dreadful. She is told that at that time there was a dancing club, a music club, and a dramatic club, and, worst of all, an itinerant troop of actors once came to town. About these things one could not, however, speak freely until Dina Dorf, Miss Bernick, and her mother had upon some pretext been induced to withdraw. Mrs. Rummel and Mrs. Holt send their daughters out of the room, and then the floodgates are opened. How these "fine and quiet ladies" enjoy the gossip which now is heard! They seem to be more interested in this than in their work for the "depraved." Of especial interest was the news that Johan Tønnesen, a brother of Mrs. Bernick, had been rather intimate with one of the itinerant actresses, Mrs. Dorf, the mother of Dina, and for this reason he had to leave for America as soon as possible. But before leaving he had supplied himself with a large sum of money from the cash box of the widow of Bernick. And Lona Hessel, his half-sister, had — just think of it! — she had followed him to America! And in America she is reported to have done things really not proper for a lady. She is said to have used men's boots in rainy weather.

And — would you believe it? — before she left, she boxed the ear of Consul Bernick when he told her that he was engaged to be married to Betty Tønnesen, the sister of Johan and half-sister of Lona. Dina Dorf was then taken into the home of Mr. and Mrs. Bernick, and they had made every effort to rear her so that she might become a respectable person, in spite of the fact that she was the daughter of Mrs. Dorf.

Now coffee is to be served on the veranda, and the ladies take their places around the coffee table. Dina excuses herself and returns into the garden room. Rector Rørlund follows her and asks why she does not wish to take her place with the rest. "Oh, they are so respectable and moral," she answers. It now appears that he loves Dina, but to save his reputation and to keep his position, he does not dare to let anyone know that he loves one whose mother was among the "morally depraved." He does, however, obtain from Dina, whose heart's desire is to get away from her present surroundings, the assurance that if circumstances should permit him to offer her his hand and heart, she would consent to marry him. This conversation must, however, be kept secret. Consul Bernick comes from his office together with Rummel, Vigeland, and Sandstad, and he tells the ladies that the railway is to be built. They cannot understand what has made the Consul change his mind. That is easily understood, the Consul explains. Last year a coast line was intended, and such a one would not benefit the "greater community." This time, however, the line decided upon is an inland route, and the intention is that it will reach the town by means of a branch line. To Rector Rørland who begins to worry about this "frequent intercourse with an immoral world," he says that he does not need to have the least fear. There is no danger threatening their small industrious place, which is resting on such a sound and moral foundation.

A telegram is brought to Consul Bernick from the shipowners of *Indian Girl:* "Make only the absolutely necessary repairs. Send *Indian Girl* over as soon as possible. Season fine; will float on its cargo if necessary." Consul Bernick is terrified: "Float on its cargo? Those men know very well that in case of a mishap the ship with such a cargo will sink like a stone. I'd like to see that shipowner of ours who would stoop to such an act. Not one, no, not a single one!"

Olaf comes rushing in to tell the company that a troop of circus riders has just landed with horses and wild animals, — and many passengers, too. This news is variously received. Some are glad to have the opportunity of seeing the riders; others do not care to see them at all, that, at any rate, is what they say.

Soon they do see these "horrid people." A lady dressed in a gray gown highly offends their sense of propriety. "Think of it! She is herself carrying her traveling bag and on her back, too." She is, of course, the manager's wife. And there is the manager himself, — the one with the long beard . . . "Don't look at him, Hilda," says Mrs. Rummel. "Don't you do it, either, Netta," says Mrs. Holt. But what is that? Both the manager and his wife throw a greeting up to them. That is going too far, indeed! Rector Rørlund makes the ladies resume their places in the garden pavilion, closes the door to the garden, draws the window shades so that the place is darkened.

But what happens? The supposed manager's wife herself enters with a greeting, even calling several of them by name! It is Lona Hessel, who has returned from America together with her brother Johan. She receives no cordial greeting. Far from it. They seem rather to be frightened, all of them, and especially Consul Bernick. This does not, however, seem to make much of an impression on Miss Hessel. She merely thinks they look very sad. And are they not seated in a dark room, sewing on something white? Can it be that the family is in mourning for the death of some dear one? Very solemnly Rector Rørlund offers the information: "My dear Miss Hessel, you are now present at a meeting of the 'Society for the Morally Depraved.'" "What are you saying? That these fine, quiet ladies are — ?" Oh, no, now she understands. — "But there must be full daylight here when the boy (Johan) comes." And she goes and draws aside the draperies. When Consul Bernick hears that Johan also has come, he apparently finds it still more difficult to conceal his anxiety.

Rector Rørlund, putting aside the book, now says: "Ladies, I do not think that we are in a frame of mind to do more work to-day. But to-morrow we may meet again."

Miss Hessel (as the visiting ladies rise to leave): "Yes, let us do as you say; I'll be present."

Rector Rørlund: "You? Permit me, Miss Hessel. What will you do in our society?" Miss Hessel: "I will give it airing."

With this answer of Miss Hessel the *Exposition* ends. It suggests what the subject of the action will be. Miss Hessel and her brother have come to give the society, and society in general, an airing. And we have already a suspicion that that is just what it needs.

II.   The Rising Action. Act II.

Since Consul Bernick is the central figure in the drama, its principal action will necessarily be directly connected with him, in such a way that he either himself performs the acts or is made the object of them.

Consul Bernick is, as already mentioned, the leading and most capable man in this little Norwegian coast town. He is also, no doubt, its richest citizen, — at any rate the one who has done the greatest and most conspicuous things for the welfare of the town. He has also the appearance of being the town's most noble, most disinterested, and most conscientious citizen, —

in short, a pillar of society without compare, the man
without a blemish and without spot. The rising action
shows what a hard fight Consul Bernick, on account of
many conflicting circumstances, now must wage to
maintain his position, and above all how desperately he
must struggle in order to maintain the appearance of
being what he is not. There are many things which
must be kept concealed. But while fighting to conceal
these things, he makes himself guilty of much which is
worse than what he wishes to conceal. The rising action is, in short, a process of hardening, which takes
place in the consul. And there are no less than ten steps
leading up to the climax in this process.

First Step.

Consul Bernick comes all out of sorts into the presence of his good kindhearted wife Betty, who would do
anything to please him. And when he finds out that
the already mentioned society did not meet the day before, as had been decided, he becomes even more ill-
humored. These fine, decent ladies are evidently beginning to feel embarrassed at meeting in his house.
And this riff-raff which has returned from America is
the cause of it! "To be saddled with them just now!
What a misfortune!" Mrs. Bernick begins to weep,
saying that she cannot help that they are related to her
nor that they have returned at this time. Consul Bernick answers that he has heard that story before, and
that if she wants to cry, she will have to leave the room.
Would she perhaps let others see her red eyes? Yes,
that would be fine, if it became known that — . . . And
Mrs. Bernick leaves the room. Shipbuilder Aune enters. He receives a severe scolding from the Consul,
because the work of repairing the *Indian Girl* is progress-
ing so slowly. The papers have begun to complain of
the rumpus caused night and day by its reckless crew.
And it is he, the Consul, who is being blamed for it. Yes,
the papers have begun even to insinuate that Consul

Bernick & Company permit the wharf hands to make ready their own ship, the *Palm Tree*, and do not concern themselves about the *Indian Girl*. And "I whose duty it is by force of example to influence my fellow citizens, must have this thrown in my teeth. This I can not tolerate. It will not do to have my name besmirched," says Consul Bernick. And just now, when he is charged with this great railway affair, he needs all the good will and esteem of his fellow citizens. For this reason Shipbuilder Aune must have the *Indian Girl* ready the day after to-morrow. "You might just as well say this afternoon," Aune answers. "The bottom of the vessel is completely rotten." Consul Bernick is well aware of this. Nevertheless he issues his ultimatum — that Aune will either have the vessel ready at the appointed time or lose his position. And poor Aune, who does not like to lose his job, leaves with the remark: "The *Indian Girl* can clear day after to-morrow," — something which would be entirely impossible without permitting dishonest repairs to be made. Consul Bernick is, however, well satisfied. "Well, if I did not make that stiff-necked fellow come to terms, after all!"

Second Step.

Hilmar Tønnesen is ever busy dinning in the ears of Consul Bernick and wife the outrageous conduct of the American relatives and the taunts that he must hear because of his relationship to them. Editor Hammer had even been so impudent as to congratulate him on "the home-coming of his rich cousin"; and in so doing he had, of course, alluded to the rich helping of money which Johan had received from the funds of old Mrs. Bernick before he left home. And these two are walking through the town in company with Dina and Olaf, in order impressively to remind people of the fact that they belong to the town's most prominent family. The coming of the visitors from America has filled Consul Bernick with terror; he is in constant fear lest, while

they are at home, mention may be made to Johan of
this theft. He can scarcely bear to see them. But just
now they are both seen to be coming with Olaf straight
toward the house, and so Consul Bernick says to his
wife: "Listen, Betty, it is my particular wish that you
show them all possible friendliness." And Consul Bernick himself will, of course, be smiling and friendly.
Naturally, one must guard his reputation, and so it can
not be helped if he must be a little hypocritical.

Third Step.

Lona and Johan begin to speak about all the evi-
dences of Consul Bernick's great beneficence which they
have seen on their walk through town. They have discovered that all the greatest and finest they have seen
are due to him. In answer to this Consul Bernick mod-
estly says: "Well, one must do his best for the community he lives in."

"But it is a real joy to see how people appreciate your
efforts," Says Lona. "I am not vain, but I could not
help reminding one or two of the people we were talking with that we belonged to the family." — "Ugh!"
says Hilmar Tønnesen.

Hilmar is momentarily left alone, and Olaf comes,
beaming with joy, to tell him that Uncle Johan had
asked him if he would like to accompany them to America. Dina and Johan have been taking a stroll together
during the morning hours, and as they enter, Dina says:
"It was splendid; I have never had such a nice walk before." But when Johan proposes that they take a walk
every day, she says: "Oh no, Mr. Tønnesen, we must
not do that." "And why not?" says he. "I will tell
you," she replies; "I am not like the other girls here.
There is something — something about me." — "Well,
but you have not done anything wrong?" "No, not I,
but — No, I will not say anything more about it. You
will surely hear about it from the others." She has,
however, a strong desire to go to America and there try

to work her way and become a respectable person. But she hopes that people over there may not prove to be so very "proper and moral," as they try to appear in her own town, but that they might be "natural." In that case it would be fine for her to be there. "Yes," says Johan, "that is perhaps what they are." But when he proposes that they make the trip together, she says: "No, I could not go with you; I would have to go alone. But believe me, I should get along."

Dina leaves the scene as Consul Bernick enters. He and Johan remain. And now we learn something very strange indeed. It was not Johan that had been guilty of the scandal with Mrs. Dorf; it was none other than that paragon of virtue, Consul Bernick. But Johan had magnanimously taken the blame upon himself and then left the country. For this service Consul Bernick now most cordially thanks him: "My house and home, my happy family life, my standing as a citizen in society — all this I owe to you."

Johan is of the opinion that, considering the circumstances, there was nothing else for him to do, and he answers: "I was free, my parents were dead; you, on the other hand, had an old mother living, and, besides, you had just become engaged to Betty, who loved you most dearly." The only thing for which he felt regret was that, in a moment of weakness, he had told his sister Lona about the whole affair. But Consul Bernick would have nothing to fear. Lona would not say anything, and Johan would take better care of his tongue another time. And as assurance, he gives the Consul his hand. Consul Bernick is glad and relieved. He will thus be able to keep on basing all that he is, all that he has, and all for which he is praised on a — lie.

Fourth Step.

In this scene we have a conversation between Johan and Miss Martha Bernick, in which we learn that while Consul Bernick is regarded to be in many ways what he is not, his sister, who is regarded as of no account, is, in fact, highly deserving. She is one of the noblest types of women portrayed by Ibsen; and that is saying a great deal. She had had some reason to believe that Johan, before he left for America, had loved her, and he, at any rate was her only love. And then he had to leave, and in such a way! She believed, however, that he would soon return, and for fifteen long years she had been waiting — and she has tried as much as possible to atone for his wrongdoing, tried to do what he ought to have done, but what he failed to do, tried to take care of Dina. "I have waited so long, Johan, — too long," she tells him. Now she understands that he has forgotten her — or perhaps never loved her.

The next episode is a conversation between Mrs. Bernick and Lona Hessel. Lona is determined to do all that she can in order to make Johan marry Dina. Mrs. Bernick is of the opinion that this would be a terrible scandal, and that Karsten "with his strict moral ideas," would never give his consent to this.

But next follows a conversation between Lona and Consul Bernick. And this is the main part of the fourth step. Here also we are given an opportunity of hearing many strange things. We are surprised to learn that Karsten Bernick was engaged to marry Lona before he met her half-sister Betty, secretly of course, for then "no one could make fun of your bad taste," says Lona.

But when he was to take charge of the business and was in need of money, he broke the engagement with Lona and married Betty, whom he did not love, but who was to receive a large inheritance, while Lona would have none at all. "But now," says Lona, "I have come home, not to execute vengeance, but to get you out of your lie; in the first place your lie to me; then the lie towards Betty; then the lie towards Johan." Consul Bernick answers that Johan has promised to keep silent, and he adds: "If any one else accuses me, I shall deny everything."

Fifth Step.

Now the storms begin to rise against Consul Bernick
from every quarter. Merchants Rummel and Vigeland
are the first to come rushing in to tell Consul Bernick
that he must, by all means come to the Council of Trade.
The entire railway project is at stake. People have begun to insinuate that private interests are hidden behind
the proposal for a line to the interior. And no amount
of explanation seems to help. No one will believe it.
Consul Bernick must come. No one will suspect him.
Rector Rørlund enters "painfully agitated," as he says,
and wants to know if it is with the Consul's knowledge
and consent that Dina Dorf appears on the street in company with a man from whom, of all others in the world,
she should be kept farthest apart. The consul says that
he knows nothing about it. Then Hilmar Tønnesen
comes on the same errand and relates that Johan Tønnesen, that horrid man, wants Dina to go with him to
America. How dreadful! All are speechless with
amazement — all except Lona, who is of the opinion
that it would be "just splendid." As Johan and Dina
enter, Rector Rørlund asks: "Answer me, Dina; is this
your intention — is it your full and free determination?" Dina answers: "I *must* get away from here."
Rector Rørlund: "But leave with him — with him?"
Dina: "Tell me of anyone else that has the courage to
set me free." Then Rector Rørlund bursts forth. He
would ill serve the community over whose manners and
morals he has been placed as a guardian, he says, that
in fact it would be inexcusable, if he should keep silent
now. And Dina should know that it was this man who
caused all her mother's misfortune and shame. And besides, it was also he who emptied the widow Bernick's
strong box. Only Lona is now able to hinder Johan
from laying violent hands on Rector Rørlund. Rørlund
continues: "And this is the truth. Consul Bernick has
said so himself, and the whole town knows it. Now,
Dina, now you know him."

Johan, who has solemnly promised Consul Bernick that he will keep silent, is thus unable to defend himself. Turning to the Consul he asks him to answer the accusations: Consul Bernick replies, "Today let there be silence."

Act III.

Sixth Step.

Act III begins as did Act II with a scene in which Mrs. Bernick is reprimanded by her husband. This time she is told that she does not care whether their boy Olaf lives or dies. Last night he went out to sea with a fishing boat, and now he threatens to run away. But he, the Consul, has work to leave behind him and can not afford to be left childless. Olaf must be kept in the house, and there is to be no arguing about it.

Manager Krap comes in and tells the Consul that Shipbuilder Aune doubtless intends to let the *Indian Girl* sink with all on board. The vessel appeared, indeed, to be repaired, but the repairs were all bogus. The ship would never reach New York. Consul Bernick feigns to be frightened but declares that he can not believe such a thing of Aune. But to make sure about it he asks Krap to make a second investigation. And if it shall prove to be as Krap has stated, they must of course report the case: "We cannot make ourselves accomplices in a crime. I must keep my conscience unspotted. And it would make a good impression on both the press and the public at large if they saw that I set aside all personal considerations and let justice take its course."

This conversation has seemingly no bearing on what is told in this part of the drama, but it has a great deal to do with what follows in the eighth scene. For that reason it will be well to remember it.

Now follows another conversation which will shed light on later situations. The professional gossip, Hilmar Tønnesen, comes and tells Consul Bernick that there is a report going about, and he has heard it at the club, that one of the lawyers of the city has been secretly commissioned to buy up all the forests, all ore deposits, all waterfalls, and so forth, all of which will be of great value when the new railway shall be completed. Consul Bernick, however, assures him that this is impossible; there is too much public spirit in the community to permit anything like that to happen.

Now follows a conversation between Bernick and Lona Hessel, and this forms the main part of the sixth step. Lona wants to know about the *theft* of which Johan has been accused. And now Consul Bernick's position is not an easy one: but he tries to clear himself as well as he can. His answer may briefly be summarized as follows: There has been no theft; not a cent has been stolen. But when he came home from his sojourn abroad and was to assume control of the business which his mother without any business ability had managed, he found that it was on the verge of ruin. It was almost impossible to meet all obligations. This became known, and as the most plausible explanation people assumed that Johan had taken the money with him. As the rumor spread the amount grew larger and larger. Says Consul Bernick: "I seized this rumor as a life buoy. The creditors were content to believe that if they granted us time, everything would be set right again. Yes, Lona, that rumor saved our house and made me the man I now am." — Lona now begins to speak to his conscience: Only by speaking out can he make atonement for the wrong he has committed. Bernick replies: "Can you ask such a thing?"

Seventh Step.

Johan enters and now he will "speak first." But only to demand that Consul Bernick shall confess, for now he "has need of the truth." But the Consul says that just now he needs that nothing be said, for only thus will he avoid losing his "moral repute." Johan is not so much concerned about the rumor of the theft, but

Consul Bernick must let people know the truth with
respect to the affair of Mrs. Dorf, for now he is going to marry Dina Dorf and live in the town. For that
reason he must have his own reputation restored. Consul Bernick answers that by confessing his guilt in that
matter he will also appear to be guilty of the theft. But
this would under the present circumstances cause his
ruin. It is no one else than he who has bought all the
tracts of land with the splendid natural resources along
the intended railway, and if this should become known,
the railway project would come to naught, and then he
would be a ruined man. But if the branch line is built,
he will become a millionaire. Only under his control
can these properties be of benefit to their community
and be a continued blessing to the many who would receive their sustenance from them. Lona is so strongly
impressed by this that she says: "Johan, after what
you have heard you must be silent and go away." Johan
promises to leave and also to keep silent: "But I shall
come again, and then I shall speak." Consul Bernick
promises to share the profits with Johan, if he will promise to leave, — and not return. "Keep your money, but
give me back my name and fame," is Johan's answer:
"I must and shall and will win Dina. So I shall sail to-
morrow with the *Indian Girl*. . . . But in two months I
shall be back again, and then the guilty one must take
the guilt upon himself." Consul Bernick answers:
"But if you speak, I shall deny all, *all!*" — Johan leaves.

Eighth Step.

Johan leaving with the *Indian Girl* is something that
at once engages the mind of the Consul. Hurriedly he
says: "Lona, you must get this stopped!" But she
answers that she has no longer any power over him,
and she leaves the room.

Shipbuilder Aune comes and he wants to know if the
Consul is determined that if the *Indian Girl* cannot sail
the next morning, he will dismiss him and ruin the

standing which he has had in his home and in the circle
of his acquaintances. The Consul replies: "Do I gen-
erally change my mind? We have discussed that
point." "Well," says Aune, "then the *Indian Girl* must
sail." After a pause the Consul asks: "You will, I suppose, assure me that the repairs are thoroughly carried
out?" Aune replies that the Consul had allowed him very
short time, but that "the weather is fine and it is mid-
summer." And though the Consul knows that the *Indian Girl* is doomed to founder, and that Johan is to be
a passenger, he says: "Yes, the *Indian Girl* sails." Aune:
"To-morrow?" Consul Bernick: "Yes!"

Ninth Step.

Manager Krap comes once more and wants to know
whether it really is the Consul's intention to let the
Indian Girl sail the next morning. He has, to be sure,
not had occasion to make any close investigation, and
the official inspectors have found nothing to complain
of. But the Consul knows, says he, that the official
inspection does not mean much, especially when it concerns a yard "with a reputation like ours." Krap is
morally certain that the *Indian Girl* will never be heard
of again, if it sails the next day. The Consul becomes angry and tells Krap that he says this because he does not
like Aune. He tells Krap that Aune has completely re-
assured him; and if the *Indian Girl* should meet with disaster, it would not be their fault, since the official inspection has found nothing to criticize. Merchant Vigeland
now enters and asks the Consul if he does not think the
Palm Tree might sail the next morning. Storm signals
have, it is true, been displayed, but the *Palm Tree* is solid
— and besides, fulled insured, and if that old hulk
Indian Girl can venture out — and with such a crew into
the bargain — it would really be a shame if they did
not let the *Palm Tree* sail. — This then is the situation:
Consul Bernick knows that the *Indian Girl* must founder
if the weather is ever so little rough. He knows that

Johan Tønnesen is to be a passenger on that ship, and
now he has heard that a storm is coming on. Nevertheless he gives orders that the *Indian Girl* may sail.

Tenth Step.

But Consul Bernick's conscience troubles him. And
now when Rector Rørlund comes, the Consul asks him
some subtle questions. Pretending to be thinking of the
railway, he says: "Suppose that blasting is necessary
in a dangerous place, and that the railway cannot be
built unless this blasting takes place. And suppose that
the engineer knows that the workman who is to light
the fuse will be killed, but it is his duty to send some
one to do it." Rector Rørlund says: "No engineer
among us would ever do that." The Consul is thinking of Johan and the *Indian Girl*, but does not find any
comfort in the answer of Rector Rørlund.

But when now Mrs. Bernick, Lona Hessel, Miss Bernick and also Johan and Dina enter, Rector Rørlund
takes occasion to tell Johan that the young woman
whom he is courting is engaged to him. This no one
believes, and Lona calls it a lie. Then Johan asks Dina
if Rørlund speaks the truth. And after a little while Dina
answers: "Yes." We know the circumstances under
which this betrothal took place. But Dina remembers
only the "yes" which Rector Rørland had once tricked
her into saying. Consul Bernick says: "Johan, you
won't sail now with the *Indian Girl?*" Johan: "Yes,
now more than ever." Manager Krap comes in and in
an aside asks the Consul: "Is it settled that the *Indian
Girl* is to sail to-morrow?" The Consul's answer is:
"She is to sail." He goes into his office.

III.   The Climax.

Manager Krap slightly opens the door to the Consul's
office and says: "Pardon me for coming again, Consul
Bernick, but there is a terrible storm brewing." He waits
a moment. There is no answer. "Is the *Indian Girl* to

sail in spite of it?" The Consul answers from his office: "The *Indian Girl* is to sail in spite of it."

IV. The Falling Action.

Act IV.

In this act a process of humiliation is presented. One charge after another is made against the conscience of the Consul, until he at last must make a confession, a full confession; and this confession forms the catastrophe. There are altogether six such charges; and these form the different scenes. But now it is not Consul Bernick who carries the main action, but he is himself the object of the action. In this act many secondary actions must also be included in our presentation.

First Scene.

In the evening of the day when the two ships are to sail Consul Bernick comes into the garden pavilion, and there he finds Merchant Rummel very busy making arrangements for a festive night. When asked by the Consul what this means Rummel answers: "It means that the proudest moment of your life has arrived. The whole town is coming in procession to do honor to its leading citizen." It is to be such a splendid affair. Hilmar Tønnesen has written a song which begins with these words: "Wave the Ideal's banner high." And Rector Rørlund is to make the principal address and Consul Bernick will reply to it. The Consul feels as if a dagger has been thrust into his heart, and he is far from relieved by the fact that Rummel tells him that the singing which they hear is on board the *Indian Girl*, which is just ready to sail. Consul Bernick tells Rummel that it will be impossible for him to take part in the celebration; he simply can not; he is sick; the celebration must be called off. Rummel answers that it is now too late to do that, and besides he maintains that this festival is really necessary. "Our opponents must be

crushed under the weight of the unanimous utterance
of public opinion; the rumors are spreading over the
town; that the properties have been purchased can no
longer be kept secret. This very evening while voices
are raised in song and speech, and glasses are clinking,
in short, amid all the effervescent festivity of the occasion, you must let them know what you have ven-
tured for the welfare of the community." Of course,
Consul Bernick will have to yield. And besides, Lona
comes to tell him that Johan's determination to sail on
the *Indian Girl* stands "firm as a rock."

In the following interludes we witness, 1. That Olaf
is leaving the house with a bundle under his arm, in order, as he says, to go down to the pier and bid Johan
good-bye. 2. That Miss Bernick is coming with Dina,
who desires to be permitted to accompany Johan to
America. And though Miss Bernick, as she later says,
"has loved Johan more than all the world," she is nevertheless assisting to remove every misunderstanding between Dina and Johan. Dina's engagement to Rector
Rørlund was, as we know, only a misunderstanding also.
Dina loves Johan and admits that she never loved Rørlund. He had taken advantage of Dina's unpleasant position in the home of Consul Bernick and caused her to
promise that, when he should find it consistent with his
dignity to make her an offer of marriage, she would accept it. Now both Dina and Johan are very happy. But
Dina says that she will not marry as soon as they arrive
in America. She will first try to make her own way, until she finds that she amounts to something. 3. Next we
have a conversation between Lona and Martha Bernick,
who now are left alone; and now, at last, we learn fully
to know these two noble women.

Second Scene.

The second assault upon the conscience of the Consul occurs during a conversation with Lona Hessel. She
begins to speak to his conscience. She wants to know

what kind of satisfaction this make-believe and deception, all this lying and hollowness can give him. Consul Bernick answers: "It gives me none. I must sink along with the whole of this bungled social system. But after us a new generation will grow up. I am working for my son. It is for him that I am preparing a life task." "With a lie as a foundation?" is Lona's query. "Consider what sort of inheritance you are giving him." To this Consul Bernick answers: "I am giving him an inheritance a thousand times worse than you know." He is evidently thinking of the sailing of the *Indian Girl* with Johan as passenger. "But now it is done. Now I must go on. You shall not succeed in crushing me!" Lona tells him that he does not need to fear for Johan. "He will never return. He is gone forever, and Dina has gone with him — to become his wife." Consul Bernick: "Gone! — she too! — in the *Indian Girl?*" Lona: "No, he dared not trust such a precious cargo to that rotten old tub. Johan and Dina sailed on the *Palm Tree.*" Consul Bernick: "Ah! — And so — in vain — !" He means that it is to no purpose that he — in order to be rid of Johan — has sent the whole crew of the *Indian Girl* to certain death. Johan did, after all, fail to sail on that ship.

Third Scene.

The third charge against the conscience of Consul Bernick is also made by Lona. She continues: "I did not come here to betray you but to stir you so as to make you speak of your own accord. In this I have failed. Remain secure in the lie. Look, I am tearing your letter to pieces. Now there is nothing to testify against you, Karsten. Now you are safe. Be happy too — if you can." Consul Bernick is deeply moved; but he answers that it is now too late; he can not live after that day. He feels so small, so very mean in comparison with these two unselfish and morally strong personalities, Lona and Johan.

Fourth Scene.

Now the action is moving with increasing rapidity. Hilmar Tønnesen comes and tells that Olaf, the Consul's only son, has sailed on the *Indian Girl*. He has sent a written notice to Hilmar with the information that he intends to hide among the cargo until they are out to sea. — Consul Bernick (staggering backwards): "Olaf — on the *Indian Girl!* I shall never see him again!"

Fifth Scene.

Just now when Consul Bernick is plunged into the darkest despair, the festal procession is approaching. He says: "I cannot, I will not receive anyone. Away with all this!"

Sixth Scene.

Consul Bernick now learns that his wife has not been such a careless mother, after all. She has been the first to find out that Olaf was gone, and having a presentiment about his intentions, she had hurried to Aune and together with him boarded the *Indian Girl* and found her son in the hold of the ship. Now she brings him in. Consul Bernick is, however, not to be permitted to see him until he gives his promise not to punish him. She also tells that Aune — in Consul Bernick's name — has revoked the sailing orders of the *Indian Girl*. And the Consul is to promise also that Aune shall not be punished. Consul Bernick: "Oh, what unspeakable happiness!" Mrs. Bernick: "You are not angry?" — Consul Bernick: "Oh, what joy! Beyond measure, Betty!"

V. The Catastrophe.

The procession may now come at any time. Consul Bernick will now be able to speak, and now he *will* speak. The procession arrives, and Rector Rørlund makes a fine speech in honor of the guest of the occasion, whom he lauds to the skies. Consul Bernick replies to the address. And now he makes a full confession. It was he who had wronged Mrs. Dorf, and Johan Tønnesen was not guilty of any theft. And with regard to the purchase of properties, rich in natural resources, along the prospective railway, he says: "These properties, all of them, I have bought — I alone. They are at present controlled by me. I have, of course, confided in my fellow-workers, Messrs. Rummel, Vigeland, and Sandstad [angry potests came from these]; but this evening I have made up my mind that shares in these properties are to be offered to anyone who may wish to be a shareholder." Many voices: "Hurrah! Long live Consul Bernick!" Lona Hessel: "Now at last you have found yourself again!" Most of the others, however, stand speechless with astonishment. — Rector Rørlund says: "What a thunderbolt! The most prominent man in town!" And soon the visitors are all gone. Tønnesen too steals away, and is heard saying: "How, after this, one is to hold high the banner of the ideal, I for one — Ugh!" Soon all the lights are extinguished, and silence reigns. But in the circle of those who remain — Consul Bernick, Mrs. Bernick, Miss Hessel, Manager Krap, and later Olaf and Shipbuilder Aune — there is happiness and joy.

Consul Bernick says: "Betty, can you forgive me?" Mrs. Bernick answers: "Do you know, Karsten, that you have opened for me the brightest hope I have had for many years? Now I shall win you." Olaf is now permitted to choose his own life work. Gladdened by this the boy says: "Thank you, father. Then I do not wish to be a pillar of society, for I think that must be very tiresome." And poor Aune has no reason to regret that he, of his own accord, kept the *Indian Girl* from sailing; for he is told that he is to continue as the Consul's co-worker. Turning to the three faithful women, Betty, Martha, and Lona, the Consul says: "And we — we have a long, earnest day of work before us, — I especially. But let it come. Only give me your support, you true and faithful women. This I have learnt in these days, that it is you women who are the pillars of society." In answer to this Miss Hessel says: "Then you have learned a poor wisdom, brother-in-law." And placing her hand on his shoulder, she adds: "No, no, the spirits of truth and of freedom — these are the Pillars of Society."

Remarks.

Now we can probably answer the question whether Ibsen has in this drama fully followed the program of naturalism. We shall have to answer both yes and no. We must admit that here he has not been smoothing matters over, but has spoken freely and candidly. He has not by any means glossed over the faults and short-comings of the society in question. As we think over the picture he has painted we must say: Here is, indeed, much need of reformation and of cultivation. But the work is surely not "swine-literature." *The Pillars of Society* may be read in any circle of listeners. But nevertheless we may not without reason call this work fully naturalistic. It does not appear that Ibsen is here attacking family life, wedlock, and religion, or that he is in doubt about their value. He does, to be sure, chastise Consul Bernick, but his fault is not that he is the father of a family; it is that he is such an incompetent one. Family and family life must consequently be of great value. And what about the state of marriage? The poet awakens our sympathy for Mrs. Bernick, because Consul Bernick marries her on account of her money. He also makes us sympathize with Miss Hessel and Miss Bernick, because they are deceived in their hope of a happy marriage. The marriage state must consequently also be of value. And what of religion? Does he question the value of it? Quite the contrary, as far as I am able to judge. He directs a scorching criticism against Rector Rørlund and the ladies who pretend an interest in missions, not because they are religious, but because they are hypocritical, — because

they are not what they pretend to be. Religion must
consequently also be of value. And what of the foundation on which Ibsen would build the new society? It
is liberty, honesty, and truth. And are not these ideas
found in the Bible? Compare the words: "The truth
shall make you free." They belong then to the cardinal
virtues of Christianity. For where, outside of Christianity do we find true liberty, honesty, and truth? I fancy
that Dr. Brandes did not feel unmixed joy in reading
The Pillars of Society.

Ibsen is from now on a naturalist in his whole method
of presenting and pointing out the sins and shortcomings of the individual as well as of society. Most clearly
is this evident in those four works which are commonly
called social dramas: *The Pillars of Society, A Doll's
House, Ghosts,* and *An Enemy of the People.*

I will not make bold enough to say that Ibsen followed
this path because it had been pointed out by Brandes. It
seems probable that Ibsen would have followed it and
would have written what he wrote and in his own way,
even if Brandes had never existed. Ibsen had even before been quite outspoken, e. g. in *The League of Youth,
Brand,* and *Peer Gynt.* And there is in his entire literary
production a definite plan from beginning to end, as
also he himself has said. There is no denying that
Brandes exerted an influence on Ibsen, but his production would, I believe, have been essentially the same
even apart from Brandes. He even bided his time even
after Brandes had appeared. Brandes came forward as
a critic in 1871, whereas *The Pillars of Society* was not
written until 1877. And in this interval of years Ibsen
had written his quantitatively greatest work, *Emperor
and Galilean.*

But why did Ibsen write *The Pillars of Society* and
what did he really mean by this work?

After a ten years' stay abroad, chiefly in Italy and
Germany, Ibsen had returned to Norway in 1874. And
he came in order to end his *exile,* as he calls this period

of his life. But in spite of this and of the fact that he was
received with great homage, he in the following autumn
once more went into *exile*. There must have been something which disturbed his peace of mind at home, something that irritated him; and there can scarcely be any
doubt that it was these things which he discussed, or
rather began to discuss in his next work, *The Pillars of
Society*.

But what are these things? Well, if I had to include
them all in one word, I should say, *hypocrisy*. If I were
allowed two words, they would be *hypocrisy* and *egoism*.
And if I were allowed three, they would be *hypocrisy*,
egoism, and *dread of the light*. But these words are, as is
easily apparent, closely related to one another in meaning. All contain the idea of insincerity or lack of love
of the truth. The lover of truth is neither a hypocrite,
nor an egoist; nor does he dread the light, for he "walk-
eth in the light."

These three evils will, as Ibsen believes, more easily
steal into a small people, like the Norwegian, and vaunt
themselves there, just because it is small and comparatively isolated. He does not, of course, mean that these
evils are not to be found in the large peoples. *The Pillars
of Society*, as well as *Brand* and *Peer Gynt*, has not only a
special but also a general purport. Its accusations are
directed against individuals as well as against social
units, large or small, but especially and primarily against
the small social unit. But for what reasons? The danger of becoming egoistic is evidently greater in a small
than in a large society. In a small community one will
never witness such great and manifest crimes as may be
perpetrated in the larger community, — for instance,
that immense fortunes are made by a few or by one individual in a short time; that a few individuals may, by
forming trusts or "corners," gain control of one or more
of the most important requisites of life and so by making millions of men pay taxes to them, in a short time
become multimillionaires. And since such conditions

are not found in the small community, it is supposed to
be better than the large. Ibsen is, however, of the opinion that there are those in the small community who
would do the same things — on a smaller scale, to be
sure; but on a larger scale also, if they only dared. And
the reason that they dare not is simply that they are
afraid of being detected. It is, of course, almost impossible to keep such a thing secret in a small group; it is
too simple and too transparent. Everybody knows
everybody else. And if such a scandal is uncovered,
what a to-do there follows! Then one's popularity and
reputation, one's power and influence are gone. If an
oil magnate donates a few millions to some charitable
enterprise and then recoups himself manifold by increasing the price of oil just a little, who would be able to
keep account of it? And even if some were able to do
so and called him a thief, what would the oil magnate
care? He is far away from his critics, keeps no company with them, and may not even know what they say
or write about him. He continues to be the great, the
rich, the mighty man. But if something similar were
attempted in a small community, even on a smaller scale,
it would be necessary to keep it secret, and the result
would be hypocrisy. The great stain on the name of
Consul Bernick was not caused by what he did in order
to become great and rich and powerful, but what he did
to keep those transactions secret. When Consul Bernick
tried to become a millionaire by his railway project, he
was, it is true, neither disinterested nor honest, even if
his actions were a matter of everyday occurence in a
large community. But what he did to keep the business
a secret was far worse. And we know what that was.
So also his affair with Mrs. Dorf. The original guilt was
bad enough, but the guilt he incurred by keeping it
secret was far worse.

And what about the dread of light? Such a dread of
the light as that which Ibsen attacks in *The Pillars of
Society* is not now very much in evidence in Norway or

in other small social units. But in the seventies the situation was different, as might be expected. We have heard of the many new ideas which were thronging in from France and England; was it strange that a small community like Norway would hesitate to give such ideas admittance? They were ideas which, if admitted, might turn upside down everything hitherto considered true and proper. But to keep out the thoughts and ideas coming from the great countries will, in the long run, be found impossible. One will always have to suffer for shutting oneself in, as in a spiritual quarantine. It will result in blindness like that of a mole. A society attempting it, will be left behind. On such an occasion it is far more profitable to follow the principle: "Prove all things; hold fast that which is good." But in the seventies it seemed to Ibsen that this principle was not followed in Norway as it should be. And for that reason he created Rector Rørlund. That this character is an exaggeration is soon apparent. Even in the seventies one could scarcely by the most diligent search have found such a mole as Rector Rørlund, and least of all was he a typical representative of the Norwegian theologian, although some might, no doubt, have resembled him to a certain degree; Henrik Jæger considers Rørlund a perfect type of the "supercilious theologian"; Gerhard Gran says: "We do not know him." What, then, is he? We shall not be far from the truth if we say that he, like the sheriff and the minister in *Brand*, is an exaggeration, almost a caricature, of the group that he is to represent. And it has doubtless been Ibsen's purpose to exaggerate, so as not to make him appear "all right."

Of course, I do not mean to say, that this accusation is not valid as far as the small communities are concerned, namely that they are more apt to be self-sufficient and to isolate themselves against new thought and ideas. But not always, nor as regards all kinds of new ideas. Even in the small group new thoughts and ideas

are born, and comparatively they are as numerous (perhaps even more so) and as valuable as those born of the
larger group.   But revolutionary thoughts and ideas in
the intellectual or the civic sphere usually arise in the
larger society.   And it is such ideas which the smaller
societies try to keep out as long as possible.   Now the
ideas which we have referred to, namely those of
Compte and Darwin and so forth, were quite revolutionary in the intellectual world.   And these were the
ideas which the Norwegians in the seventies tried to
keep out, but without success.   Long before the seventies were at an end there were professors at the university (J. E. Sars among them) who had attached themselves to the new movement.

About Merchant Vigeland, Jæger says: "His type is
found in every coast town"; Gerhard Gran says: "We
know him not."   The same disagreement is also found
with regard to Consul Bernick.   And again the truth is
probably half-way between these extremes.   Gran will
surely not deny that there are many who resemble Consul Bernick, who remind us of him; but it must be admitted that one will scarcely find a Norwegian business
man of such saintly appearance who at heart is such an
unmitigated scoundrel as he.

But even if Ibsen has not been quite so successful
with regard to his types as in his next drama, *A Doll's
House*, where Helmers and Nora and Krogstad — in fact
all the characters — are as lifelike as any living person
in Norway or other civilized country, still we must not
assume that this drama, which applies the lash to the
small social unit, is a failure.   It is not so good as it
might have been if the characters had been quite true to
type, but we must admit that there is also a great deal
of truth in its fundamental idea, which is that the small
society has nothing to boast of over against the large.
While the latter may have more and often greater faults,
which are absent in the former, it is nevertheless true

that hypocrisy and dread of the light will more easily find an entrance into the small community.

Ibsen has in this work given a classic representation of hypocrisy. Henrik Jæger says that hypocrisy has never been described so well since Moliere created Tartuffe. Ibsen's representation of gossip in this drama is also classic. These very decent, very truthful, and very philanthropic ladies who are all afire with the love for the "morally depraved" and who are so very desirous of helping them, are in reality fired with the desire of reviling everything and everybody who are not just like them. And when they have given vent to their ill will, they make believe that what they have said has been prompted by their concern for one of the ladies who is not so well acquainted with conditions as they themselves are. And we shall not leave out the one whose sole interest in life is gossip, — the good-for-nothing Hilmar Tønnesen.

That gossiping is a fault peculiar to the small community we may easily understand by comparing conditions in a small town with those of a large city.

The foregoing remarks have dealt with this work in general. There are, however, a few things worth noticing in particular: first of all the conduct of Consul Bernick himself in the matter of his railway project. The situation we know. One year there is some talk of building a railway along the coast. Consul Bernick works against this, tooth and nail, for it would hurt the steamship traffic in which he himself is heavily interested. Consequently, he would suffer the greatest pecuniary loss by the building of a coast line. But, of course, he cannot use this as an argument against the project. Oh, no, he pretends that his only concern is the moral welfare of the town. The next year there is some talk of an inland railway. Consul Bernick finds that a branch line may easily connect this with the city. And along this branch line are many valuable natural resources: there are forests, ore deposits, waterfalls, and so forth. He goes to work and secretly buys up these properties at a small price. Those from whom he bought them received what they asked, no doubt, and what the properties were worth at the time. He now makes every effort to have this branch line built. In short: the original owners received what they had asked. Consul Bernick must make the greatest effort to secure the building of the railway. And when the line shall have been built, the town will not suffer, but will benefit by the fact that these properties will have been transferred to Consul Bernick. For he is the man who knows how to manage them so that they may be of benefit to the community. But these transactions Consul Bernick finds must by all means be kept secret. People must not be informed of the fact that it is primarily the Consul himself who will profit by the building of this branch line, and that he thereby may become a millionaire.

In a large community such a transaction would as a rule attract little attention. No one has suffered any loss. The one who had promoted this undertaking would be considered a financial genius. Such a transaction takes place in a large society; it is one of its great faults. Henrik Jæger says: "This action of Consul Bernick is the most natural thing in the world." True enough. But may we for that reason justify it? Was it considerate, disinterested, honest? By no means. And for that reason it is condemned, morally or ethically. Instead of being a "pillar of society" Consul Bernick is by this action shown to be an egoist. Society must support him. He makes use of it to his own advantage, and that cannot be ethically correct.

But what should he have done? If one by this question thinks of the practical management of the matter, it is perhaps not so easily answered. But theoretically it is easy enough. He should, in the first place, not have acted in an underhanded way and in secret. He should, in the second place, have done in the first place as he in his confession offered to do: to arrange it so that all who assisted in making the properties so immensely valuable would receive their just share. These would, first, be the original owners, and then, all who assisted in bringing about the building of the railway, and in this adjustment Consul Bernick would especially be taken into consideration. We are all agreed that he ought to receive a larger share than the rest.

And now just one more observation. Several of the accusations that might justly have been directed against Norwegian society in the year 1877 cannot justly be advanced against it at present. Let me mention only two of the most conspicuous examples: 1: The position of women. I do not know whether in this respect conditions were any worse in Norway at that time than in other countries. I am inclined to think that the opposite was the case. But we know that the Norwegian women now possess the same rights as men, both with regard to obtaining an education and as far as civic and political rights are concerned. The only office which a woman may not fill is that of a minister of the gospel. She has the same privilege as the man to enroll as a student in any of the institutions of learning, and she has made good use of it. In the first part of the eighties there was no female student at the university; at present one may find women in almost every class; in some classes they are even in the majority. 2. As regards what we have called "dread of the light," or the exclusion of new ideas. No one can now accuse the Norwegian society of this. There is rather more reason to complain of the opposite — that the door is too soon thrown wide open to almost all kinds of new thoughts and ideas — and, perhaps, especially so in the domain of theology.

ERRATA.

Page 19: Wergeland, read Welhaven.

Page 38: desides, read decides.

Page 86: jammer bringende, read
          jammerbringende.

Page 109: Caption 2 should precede line be-
          ginning "But the pastor," etc.